IRISH CRIMES OF

PASSION

Killing for Love Lust and Desire

BY

LIAM COLLINS

First published in 2005 by

Mentor Books
43 Furze Road,
Sandyford Industrial Estate,
Dublin 18.
Republic of Ireland

Tel. +353 1 295 2112/3   Fax. +353 1 295 2114
e-mail: admin@mentorbooks.ie
www.mentorbooks.ie

A catalogue record for this book is available
from the British Library

ISBN: 1-84210-296-6

Cover by Anú
Editing, design and layout by Mentor Books

Printed in Ireland by ColourBooks

CONTENTS

*To reporters and
those who talk to them*

1

INSIGHTS

How can a person's disappointment – stemming as it did from an unattainable dream – conceivably weigh more heavily than the most important person in his life?

Henning Mankell

The young couple who came with their two mischievous boys to run Sean Kelly's shop in the small Co Westmeath village of Castledaly in early 1999 seemed a normal happy family, getting their feet on the first rung of life's long and treacherous ladder. She was Debbie Whelan, a bright, outgoing and attractive young woman originally from Portarlington, Co Laois. He was a Dubliner, Gregory Fox.

They married young and went to live in River Forest, a big housing development in Leixlip on the outskirts of Dublin. They had their first baby quickly and a second boy soon came along.

Greg had a company called Fox Distribution Limited which aimed to get concessions for products and supply them to shops around the country. He had great plans but they didn't exactly work out as he'd hoped. However, by 1999 he had enough money and business expertise to buy the small shop and petrol station in Castledaly, about eight miles from the town of Athlone.

By this time Trevor was nine and Cillian, seven. The boys went to the local school, while Debbie ran the shop and filling station. Greg, a restless businessman, was scouting for other business opportunities, in between helping Debbie when he was needed.

On a Friday night after they put the boys to bed they went down to Fitzgerald's pub in the village for a few social drinks. Life seemed to have reached the stage where they should have been happy and content, rearing the two boys and enjoying a decent standard of living. But beneath this veneer of respectability and normality the Foxes' marriage was falling apart. Sitting in the corner of the pub, there was an edge to Debbie Fox's voice as she told her husband that it was over, she was leaving him for another man and she would be taking the boys.

Greg's reaction, at first, was calm and rational. He told Debbie he loved her, that they could get over this. He appealed to her, for the sake of the boys, to stay and work out their difficulties together. If he raised his voice, it wasn't heard above the usual pub chatter. But inside it consumed him. He really did love her. He didn't intend to lose her.

That night, after they left the pub, Gregory Fox went home and slaughtered his entire family, and then tried to kill himself.

First he went into the kitchen where Debbie was making herself a cup of tea before going to bed. He smashed a beer bottle off the wall and slashed her with the jagged remains. The gruesome attack continued when he grabbed a kitchen knife and stabbed her. After that he got one of the boys' hurley sticks and beat her over the head with it.

Gregory Fox left his wife dead, or dying, in the kitchen and went into the bedroom where his nine-year-old son was sleeping. He stabbed him thirty-one times. With blood streaming down his hands he moved to the other bedroom and stabbed seven-year-old Cillian sixteen times. Both boys had defensive wounds, indicating they had woken up as their father stabbed them.

By the time his killing frenzy had abated, Fox's entire family was dead. He then went into his own bedroom, took a handful of pills and slashed his wrists with the knife and lay down to die.

The following morning, the last Saturday of July, 2001, when the little village shop failed to open, neighbours became concerned that the family might have been robbed. They alerted the gardaí who broke in to the bungalow attached to the shop and filling station. What they found was a scene of utter blood lust.

Greg Fox didn't die. He tried to explain the savage events of the night he wiped out his family.

> I loved the three of them. I loved my wife. She didn't love me. She was going to leave. I pleaded with her not to go. I only killed the kids because I didn't want them to wake up in the morning to see that.

There seems no rational explanation why an ordinary, hard-working man would suddenly turn into a monster. He couldn't really explain it himself. But his wife's decision to leave him was the catalyst for three brutal and tragic murders.

Killing his wife because she was going to leave him is almost a rational decision, despite how wrong it is, but to slaughter two little children sleeping innocently in their beds beggars belief.

Fox lived to tell the tale but many others involved in 'crimes of passion' don't survive it themselves.

Social Psychologist, Susan Weir, reflecting on the theme of crimes of passion, says:

> Usually, the person has never committed any crime before the murder, and where one spouse has killed the other they will often commit suicide afterwards, which is not typical of other murderers.
>
> Research shows that financial pressures and stress at work are frequently part of the stresses which the person committing a crime of passion may be experiencing at the time. I believe most of us, given the extenuating circumstances and the triggers, are capable of doing the same thing.

This is the most striking feature of a crime of passion: the ordinariness of it all. These dreadful crimes are invariably carried out by people who have never done anything really violent in their lives before. Many of them are model citizens who wouldn't like to get a parking ticket. Yet for a few terrifying moments they lose complete control and go absolutely berserk. Their crime involves extraordinary levels of violence and afterwards many of the perpetrators make no attempt to disguise their guilt. They either kill themselves or they hand themselves over to the authorities. In many ways it is the opposite to real crime.

After shooting dead his girlfriend Bernadette O'Neill, Declan Lee stood in a farmyard in the cold dawn of an October morning and shot himself.

'My heart is broke. I intended to join Bernie,' he said, after surviving with horrific injuries.

In that case the former Irish attorney general and an eminent senior counsel, John Rogers, pleaded for leniency because, he said, passion sometimes makes people do things they never intended and will always regret.

> There are no criminals here, just decent people gone astray. When the truth was finally bared to him he lost control. Passion makes us do crazy things. Bitter love caused this. Do not visit on these families a verdict of murder, or it will be bitterness to live forever.

His plea was eloquent and successful: the killer received a very lenient sentence. The execution of a 'crime of passion' seems to give some people an extraordinary latitude to kill those they claim to love and get away with light sentences.

When they emerge from prison shortly afterwards to start their lives anew, their 'loved ones' are condemned to a cold grave and their families to a lifetime of torture and regret.

According to Dr Art O'Connor, who was a senior psychiatrist in the Central Mental Hospital in Dundrum which deals with many of those who are deemed 'guilty but insane', there is a 'jilted lover' syndrome.

> They adopt a position of, 'If I can't have you nobody else will. I can't live without you and I won't let anybody else live with you.' This causes an explosive mixture which, if given time, wears out. But if a shotgun happens to be handy it usually ends in death.

In France a crime of passion was recognised as two noblemen fighting for the attentions of a lover. They would square up to each other in a duel and the man left standing would get the woman. The loser would most likely be dead. But the Irish variation seems to be to kill the woman, and even the children.

Fintan Tuohy and Nuala McEvaddy were both from Ballinasloe but living in Galway city where he was a construction worker and she was a nurse's aide. Twenty-nine-year-old Nuala had a two-year-old child by another man and had been going out with twenty-six-year-old Tuohy for a couple of months. But when she broke it off because she was fed up with his jealous rages and controlling way, he wouldn't accept it. He started stalking her and made her life a misery.

Susan Weir maintains,

> Typical behaviour of an extremely jealous
> person is to indulge in unbearable, inquisitional
> cross-questioning, asking their partner where
> they have been, who they've been with, to go
> rooting through their pockets for unexplained
> receipts and so on.

At the other end of the scale the jealous person is also tormented.

> The jealous person can put themselves through
> hell, with fantasies of their spouse having sex
> with another person.

Of course, sometimes they are right but other times it is just their over-fertile imagination misinterpreting an innocent friendship or some flirting. Either way they end up killing the person they claim to love.

That is what happened one night when Fintan Tuohy followed Nuala McEvaddy back to her apartment in The Elms, a new block of apartments a few minutes walk from the centre of Galway. He was carrying a double-barrelled shotgun hidden under his coat.

First he pleaded with her to go out with him again. When she refused he grabbed her by the hair, pulling lumps of it from her head. He swung his shotgun and hit her with the butt, knocking her to the floor. Consumed with jealousy and rage he then fired a shot into the ceiling. But he emptied the second chamber into Nuala McEvaddy's head as she cowered on the floor beneath him pleading for her life. He reloaded the weapon, put the barrel under his chin and pulled the trigger. They were found lying together just inside the door of the apartment.

He would rather be bound to her in death than separated from her in real life. Psychologist Patricia Redlich wrote in the *Sunday Independent* about this crime of passion.

> Fintan Tuohy didn't have to break in. Ex-lovers seldom do. It's hard to avoid letting someone in your door, when he has already been in your bed.

> Almost invariably women have to face down the man who is obsessed. Not because they want to, but because they have no choice. We only hear about it on the rare occasions such as this one, when things go badly wrong.

> He doesn't want the love affair to be over, so he refuses to accept what she says. He may threaten suicide, grovel in tears at her feet, write endless lovelorn letters, ring her friends and family repeatedly, follow her around, beat up her new boyfriend, beg and cajole and threaten her. What he's really doing is bullying her. Like all bullies it simply doesn't work. At a more psychological level, he has to be forced to face reality.

> Men have to face their bullying ex-lovers too.

What they find most difficult is the social embarrassment of it all. Women have the added problem of real physical fear.

Women and men invariably try to run away, physically and emotionally. They hope that if they hide, avoid, placate, appease, the ex-lovers will see the light. They don't.

Women aren't foolish or foolhardy in such situations and they are always afraid. They try to play it safe, seek always to have others around, know the danger of being on their own and cornered. Sometimes they meet the unexpected, or are simply confronted with an unmanageable situation. Then they get hurt, or even murdered.

The problem is not a deficit of skills in dealing with a difficult ex-lover. It's not the woman's fault. The problem lies in the nature of love, and our attitudes to sex. If a lover is not passionate, we have difficulty believing he really loves us pale creatures who cannot ignite real love. We experience lack of passion as a real loss.

It is also difficult, if not impossible, in the early days of a love affair, to distinguish between possessiveness and loving interest, between jealousy and genuine attachment. We like it when he rings every night and asks us where we've been. We're flattered that he wants to spend all his time with us. We can't foresee where love ends and obsession begins. It only becomes apparent as the relationship progresses and by then it is usually too late.

Sex and ownership are still inextricably interwoven in many men's minds. In fact love and ownership are still inextricably interwoven in many men's minds. Whether there is any sex happening or not, they find it difficult if not impossible to be one of many. They can't accept that their woman has a right to pack her bags and go.

Such possessiveness, or jealousy, is often fuelled by lack of self-confidence, potentially combustible when sex is involved. The man is convinced that he has been tried and found wanting by his lover and that's why she's moving on. He can't handle the sense of inadequacy, or is distraught at the thought of having to make it on his own.

Sexual guilt also plays a role. They've done something wrong; she enticed him into it in true biblical fashion and now she's leaving. His anger and distress, held in check while he still enjoyed the pleasures of the forbidden, now spill over.

Of course it isn't always the man who is the obsessive. Beautiful Susan Christie was a nineteen-year-old UDR rookie when she met up with dashing Captain Duncan McAllister, a British officer with the Royal Signal Corps who was stationed near Belfast. But after they began an affair he turned out to be no gentleman.

> He told me it was obvious that I fancied him and said that he felt the same way about me. I was very attracted to him, but he was married and I wasn't sure what I wanted. As the months went by he was all I ever thought about. I had never felt this way about anyone in my life.

They met at the sub-aqua club he ran. Flirting outrageously with his sexy young trainee he chipped away at her resistance over several months. Finally she gave in and offered the married man her virginity.

They couldn't keep their hands off each other. They made love on the shores of Belfast Lough, in McAllister's 'married quarters' at the barracks, and under water in the blue-green waters of the Ascension Islands where they went on an underwater diving expedition.

'My lust for Susan was based on pure animal desires,' he said, explaining away this enjoyable interlude with a young woman whose resistance he had calculatedly broken with his promises of romance and sex.

His wife of five years, Penny McAllister from Wiltshire in England, knew nothing of the affair. She came to Ireland with her husband and got involved in community activities but what she really liked was the country life and the solitary walks in Drumkeeragh Forest with her pair of Gordon setters.

Warning bells began to sound for Captain Duncan McAllister when his lover became pregnant. He told her she had two options – an abortion and their affair could continue, or she could have the child and he would have nothing more to do with her. She chose the abortion, which he paid for.

But the dashing captain knew that his marriage would be over if word of his passionate affair ever leaked to his wife. He encouraged Susan Christie to apply for an officer course at the Royal Military Academy Sandhurst. He made sure she got it.

Without telling her, he applied for a posting in Germany, which he was also granted. The clever captain was full sure that he would get away from the jealous and possessive 'Greenfinch' Susan Christie, leaving her nothing but the memories of their sexual encounters.

His posting to Germany came through on Wednesday, March 13, 1991. McAllister phoned Susan and arranged to meet her for lunch. He told her the news and was straight with her. It was the end of the affair. He would be leaving Ireland. She seemed to take it well.

But the following weekend she took a carving knife and began honing it until the glinting steel was sharp as a razor. Who would be the victim – the cheating Captain Duncan McAllister, perhaps?

Susan Christie arranged to meet Penny McAllister for a walk in the woods one afternoon a couple of days before she was to go to England for her training. There was nothing unusual about it, the two women had become good friends. But would Susan tell Penny about her sexual exploits with McAllister?

Walking along the forest path enjoying the views and sounds, Susan pretended that her shoelace had opened. As she knelt down she drew out the deadly blade she had been hiding and suddenly ran at the innocent figure walking in front of her. Using techniques that she had been taught in unarmed combat training, she grabbed the unsuspecting Penny McAllister from behind and slit her throat, almost decapitating her. Then, in a bungling attempt to disguise her 'crime of passion', she tore her knickers and stabbed herself in the thigh, before staggering out of the woods claiming that she and Penny McAllister had been attacked as they walked there.

Detectives were puzzled why Susan Christie had so much of her 'friend's' blood on her clothes and when Captain McAllister admitted his affair four days later they knew that his wife had been killed by his lover in a jealous rage.

'I would say that I killed Penny for Duncan,' admitted Susan Christie. 'I meant to get Duncan for myself. I was that much in love with him that I would have done anything.'

'She had reached the stage where she regarded the captain's wife as an obstacle and she was determined to remove that obstacle,' said John Creaney, QC prosecuting.

Clearly sympathetic, Lord Justice Kelly asked the jury in his closing remarks in the case: 'Can you conceive of a girl of her background sharpening a knife and carrying out this vicious act of killing if she had not taken leave of her senses?'

Unlike Ireland, the British courts recognise the crime of 'Guilty of manslaughter with diminished responsibility'. Its intention is to recognise crimes of passion, rather than the discredited Irish solution of 'Guilty but insane', which means a person is technically not guilty and can be released at any time if a psychiatrist decides they are mentally stable again. Susan Christie was found guilty of this crime of 'diminished responsibility'.

'You will still be a young woman when you are released from prison. I hope that you will find some degree of happiness which has eluded you so far,' said Lord Justice Kelly, sentencing the vicious killer to five years in prison.

As she had already served fifteen months since her arrest Christie was out of jail in a little over three years.

'The bitch should have been put away for ever,' said Captain Duncan McAllister, failing to realise, perhaps, that but for the fact that he had encouraged her for his own venal pleasures she would never have killed anyone and would probably have lived life as a model citizen.

It is when love becomes corrupted into obsession that the trouble begins. One psychiatrist, speaking as an expert witness in a Dublin court, even went so far as to claim that by the victim telling her boyfriend she was leaving him and naming her new lover, 'it was as if she had fired the first bullet'. Of course, it is a defence lawyer's job to get his client off but such a claim is a dangerous distortion of a person's right to fall out of love.

What drove John Gorman of Saggart, Co Dublin, to kill his wife Martina and his eight-year-old daughter Sarah Jane with an axe on a pleasant May afternoon? John Gorman had been treated for anxiety and alcoholism for more than ten years but had beaten the drink and become an active member of Alcoholics Anonymous. Having been unemployed for years he had just got himself a reasonably good job in a timber yard.

He gave up the job one day, went home and out of the blue he slaughtered his family. Afterwards he cycled from the village where they lived along the Naas dual carriageway in heavy early morning traffic before throwing himself in front of a truck and taking his own life. In his case it was probably an act of temporary insanity, but what caused it?

'It would not be productive for you to look into the reasons why this happened,' said the coroner at the inquest. 'I don't think we will ever know why this terrible tragedy occurred.'

But of course we should try to find out why fathers, and sometimes mothers, feeling they are wronged, not only murder their spouses but also take their children on their own journey to oblivion and death.

The case of Stephen Byrne of Kilkenny is a classic example. An ordinary man, living an ordinary life, is so traumatised by a text message on his wife's mobile phone that he murders her and then drowns their two young children and himself. He believed the text message was sent by her lover and confirmed she was having an affair.

The murder of his wife would have happened in a flash of

uncontrollable anger and temper. But what happened later, the long drive through the night to the Wexford coast where all three drowned, was a deliberate act of extreme violence. While the initial act was undoubtedly a 'crime of passion' the murder of the two young boys was a gross and calculated crime of selfishness.

But people don't seem to want to know why. It is as if this particularly Irish kind of killing is the last taboo.

'The incidence of killing children has become one of the most prominent forms of homicide in this state,' said security correspondent and crime journalist Jim Cusack after a series of such cases as Stephen Byrne and Gregory Fox.

But so far no real research has ever been concluded which would give us an insight into the mind of someone who kills their children in some sort of warped revenge on their wife or lover. In fact all the evidence points to the authorities trying to cover it up in the same way as years ago they covered up suicide to protect families from the shame it was supposed to bring on them from the community.

Of course not all crimes of passion are spur of the moment flashes of anger, where a carving knife or a shotgun happen to be handy.

Joseph Robb, the son of a Belfast plumber, a graduate of Trinity College Dublin and a member of the city's caring Simon Community, seemed to have it all. Having emigrated to Canada, he had amassed a multi-million dollar fortune by the age of forty-one and become president of Northern Fine Foods, one of that country's biggest retail outlets.

He met his wife, Sheila, in Trinity College where they became lovers. When she got pregnant they decided to emigrate to Canada. The Robbs had two children. While Joseph Robb was climbing the corporate ladder, his intelligent wife was a stay-at-home mother taking care of the family. Then, at the age of thirty-two, she decided to re-start her career with a major Toronto public relations firm.

Her boss Michael Horton helped her and encouraged this talented and highly motivated mother in her new career. The two couples, Joseph and Sheila Robb, and Michael Horton and his wife Margaret, became firm friends, dining in expensive restaurants and going on exotic holiday breaks and business trips together.

But to Sheila her husband was a grey retail executive, who buried his life in his accounts and drove a safe and staid Volvo car. She wanted excitement in her life, and Michael Horton provided that. He was a dashing advertising executive who knew everybody in town, lunched with the right people and had a zest for life and love and gossip. He knew how to treat a woman.

They began a torrid affair. He wrote her love letters and bought her presents and despite his busy schedule he managed to find time for their clandestine trysts.

But after about a year he was posted to London, where he went with his wife. Sheila Robb was head-hunted to a new company and was one of the rising stars in her profession.

Now, after having had a taste of the good life, she decided she wanted to start all over again – without her husband.

Joseph. She sat him down one night and told him she was leaving him. They talked all night and while she didn't reveal the name of her lover, she made her husband sufficiently suspicious for him to go looking for evidence of an affair.

Searching through her things he found her love letters and was shocked and bewildered to find out that not only was she having an affair, but it was with a man whom he regarded as a friend. It was a double disloyalty.

Robb rang Michael Horton in London and said he was coming over, could they meet. Horton agreed to see the aggrieved lover in his hotel suite but something must have been niggling at him because, after making the arrangement, he phoned Sheila Robb from London to ask how her husband had found out. He also wanted to know how he was taking it, and if he was likely to fly into a violent rage.

She told him, no, he wasn't like that. Robb was a dull, plodding businessman. He would state his case and leave quietly. She was right, up to a point.

Joseph Robb was quite reasonable. 'Please,' he pleaded, 'give her up. She's the only woman I've ever loved.'

'I gotta go, I've a busy schedule,' answered Michael Horton and laughed in his former friend's face.

Joseph Robb picked up a bottle and smashed it into the back of the advertising executive's head. He then clubbed him a number of times before taking out a penknife he used for sharpening pencils and stabbed him twenty-two times. While Robb was explaining to the police over the phone what he'd done, Horton bled to death on the carpet of the hotel suite.

When the case was heard at the Old Bailey in London Joseph Robb's forty-one years on earth were described by the judge as 'an immaculate, honest, hard-working life stemming from relatively humble origins to commercial success.'

His wife Sheila took the brunt of the blame for what the judge described as her 'disgusting affair'. A jury found Joseph Robb not guilty of murder, but guilty of manslaughter after the judge told them it was 'a classic case of provocation'. Robb got three years in prison.

Writing about the case of the Robbs and the Hortons, clinical psychologist Maureen Gaffney said,

> Many wives feel bored and dissatisfied with their relationships but fail to convince their husbands that there is a problem. An awful lot of husbands bury themselves and their insecurities in their work and won't accept that their marriages are in trouble until their wives literally walk away.
>
> When it comes to confronting our demons most of us back down, back out, get sense or get lucky. We close the enchanted door firmly on all the emotional chaos and hang on to normality by our fingertips. But our hearts must go out to those who lose that fragile grip.

In most of these cases of crimes of passion that is exactly what it is, a fragile grip. The thin line between genius and madness, between love and despair, between life and death. As the poet

Louis MacNeice wrote: 'As the killer is close one moment / To the man he kills.'

There is a split second when a blazing row becomes total devastation as one partner kills the other and in the aftermath possibly takes their own life or the lives of others. Do our hearts go out to them? Well, maybe some. Others we cannot always find it in our hearts to forgive.

2

THOSE GORDON GIRLS

She opened the door and walked into the familiar smoky
village pub. Mrs Bergin was polishing glasses down the bar
and the barmaid was putting the finishing touches to a pint of
Guinness. Philomena Gillane's usual smile turned sour when
she saw her young husband, Pat, red faced and already tipsy,
swaying in the throng of revellers.

'What'll you have, Phil?' he bawled, as she approached
them.

'Nothing,' she answered, with an edge of anger creeping
into her voice. 'Come out to the car.'

'Arrah go on, have a drink,' Pat Gillane pleaded, his words
slightly slurred. Other people in the group, enjoying the
beginning of the Christmas festivities, muttered agreement.

'I don't want a drink, Pat,' she repeated forcefully. 'Come
on out.'

'Jaysus can't you see I'm here with the lads?' he answered,
playing the hard man in front of the men ranged along the
counter, talking of horses and football and the gossip of the
neighbourhood. It had been like this for a while now, his
drinking, and she was just sick of it.

Phil drew back her arm and the sudden slap across her

husband's rosy cheek echoed around the bar like a gunshot on a frosty May morning.

'I'll take everything you have,' Philomena Gillane warned in a loud, spiteful voice before she turned and stalked from the place, leaving her husband embarrassed and ashamed.

Phil sat back into the Opel Kadette car and drove on the winding road through the village of Caltra in east Galway and up the long potholed avenue to Beechlawn House. The big old Georgian four-storey farmhouse was home to the extended Gordon family. There was Nora 'Nonie' Gordon, the matriarch of the clan, her sons Paddy and Martin who worked the land, and her daughters Philomena and Bridie. Bridie was a barmaid at Bergin's public house in Mount Bellew. Nonie's eldest daughter, Mary, was also a barmaid and lived in Mountmellick, Co Laois.

Although Beechlawn House passed for a 'big house' in the locality, the Gordons were not a wealthy family. Nonie Gordon's husband, Michael, had died when the children were young. She had a tough time rearing her five children.

When Philomena married Pat Gillane he moved into the house and they now had a twenty-week-old son, John Michael, the apple of his grandmother's eye. Forty-one-year-old Philomena was nearly ten weeks pregnant with their second child and up to now had turned a blind eye to her husband's drinking, his fits of temper and his lies. She desperately wanted this second child, he didn't.

Pat Gillane stumbled through the front door later that night and they were waiting up for him in the big country kitchen. 'He was very drunk; he nearly broke the door down,' according to Bridie Gordon.

But it wasn't just the drink that enraged him. Pat Gillane could no longer bear the tangled web of love and deceit that was going on under the roof of the old stone farmhouse.

Suddenly the air in the old kitchen turned thick with accusation.

'The Gordons of Mishla, you think you're all high and mighty,' he slurred at his wife. Then he announced that he had been conducting an affair with her younger sister, Bridie. His tongue loosened by the drink, he described their nights of passion under the roof of that very house when she was away working in Dublin. He told her about their torrid, sex-filled weekends before and after he had married her.

'Is it true?' was all Phil could ask, shocked to the core at this betrayal by her own sister.

When Bridie admitted all, Philomena cursed her with a string of abuse.

That Christmas in 1993 came and went in Beechlawn House but the family would never be the same again. In the weeks that followed, Phil forgave her flighty younger sister for her fling, but now she looked at her husband with loathing and anger.

Thirty-two-year-old Pat Gillane had known hard and lonely days, scrabbling to make a living on a small farm and supplementing his meagre income as a jobbing lorry driver. His marriage to the older woman had given him a taste for the good things in life and the social standing he had found living here with the Gordons. Nobody was going to take 'everything he had'. He'd worked too hard for what he had; blood would be spilt before he would let anyone take it from him. In the long winter evenings the insecurity began to gnaw at him.

On a May morning in 1994 Philomena Gillane dressed quickly, throwing on a jumper and skirt over some of her night clothes. She had trained as a cook in Cork, and for nineteen years she had worked in St Columcille's Hospital in Loughlinstown, in south Co Dublin. She worked one week on and one week off, and when she was off she came back to Beechlawn House.

It was 6.40 a.m. when she opened the big front door and descended the four granite steps to the yard where her Opel Kadette car was parked. The country air was already filled with the noise of nesting crows in the tall trees around the house.

The rest of the world may have seemed to be sleeping, but unknown to her, prying eyes were watching as the pregnant mother piled her stuff onto the front passenger seat of the car. Philomena was oblivious to the unseen stalker, her mind on her precious nine-month-old son John Michael sleeping soundly upstairs in the rambling old house.

Pat Gillane, his brother Kevin and their five sisters grew up on a small farm outside Gort, Co Galway. Pat and Kevin got the farm after their parents died but to support themselves Pat worked as a lorry driver and Kevin as a council worker. One afternoon in early 1991 Pat Gillane had a couple of hours to kill in Dublin while waiting for a load and went into the Merchant pub in Winetavern Street in the city centre to pass the time and have a mineral. While he was there he fell into conversation with a girl called Philomena and her blonde friend.

Phil obviously made an impression because that casual conversation came straight back to him when he walked into O'Donoghue's pub in Fanore, Co Clare, during the Matchmaking Festival the following October. The festival is a place where country farmers go after the harvest to look for a wife. It's a tradition going back into the dark past and is organised around the spa in Lisdoonvarna and a circuit of tea dances.

On the first day of the festival Pat Gillane had eyes only for Philomena Gordon after he spotted her across the dance floor. They danced and talked for the whole time until 7 p.m. when the dancing moved back into the town of Lisdoonvarna. Pat Gillane was more eager for Philomena than she was for him, because when she wouldn't give him her telephone number he scribbled his sister's number on the back of a matchbox and handed it to her.

A couple of weeks later they met again at a showband dance in the village of Kiltormer, Co Galway, and 'that's when it started' he recalled. Philomena had a boyfriend in Dublin, a carpenter and a 'quiet lad', but she and Pat were soon lovers and in 1993 she told him she was pregnant. Within weeks they were engaged to be married.

But unknown to Philomena her fiancé had embarked on a

series of affairs, the most shocking of which was conducted under her own roof with her younger sister. Bridie Gordon was a good-looking and fun-loving girl who enjoyed the attention Pat showered on her, although she would deny this when it came back to haunt her and the Gordon family.

'I don't know why they lived in Beechlawn House. I had no say,' said Bridie. 'I had an affair with him, misfortunately. I went out with him before they got engaged. He kept pestering me and forcing himself on me,' said Bridie, explaining how the affair began.

Pat Gillane insisted that Bridie was 'throwing herself' at him and that she wanted him to leave her sister and move away with her. Whatever the truth of these different versions, Bridie Gordon went with her brother-in-law to the Rose of Tralee festival in early September, 1992. He was still having sex with the two sisters when, on April 30, 1993, the pregnant Philomena and Pat Gillane were married at a small family wedding in Knock, Co Mayo.

Marriage didn't seem to have any effect on Pat's relationship with his lover, Bridie. Only a few months after the wedding he took her to the Matchmaking Festival in Lisdoonvarna, where he had met Phil two years previously. They stayed in a hotel and had a torrid weekend of drink and sex.

'I felt what I was doing was very wrong to her,' admitted Pat Gillane. 'She didn't deserve these things. It was troubling me.' But he said he felt 'trapped' in a marriage to Philomena and still 'fancied' Bridie. She was 'always shoving herself at me,' he said. And in the big old house there was plenty of room for their love-making without disturbing the rest of the household.

But the strain was beginning to show in the Gordon household. 'I went down on my knees crying to Philomena, begging her to leave Beechlawn House, but she refused,' said Pat Gillane, claiming it was the only way he could be released from his obsession with Bridie Gordon. 'Phil said her mother would not agree,' he said, so he continued with both sisters.

Phil and Nonie were particularly close. They had gone on a trip to the United States together a few years previously and now the old woman doted on her only grandchild. She looked after him like a mother when Phil was off working her week in Dublin. When Phil was home they were like a pair of sisters going everywhere together. Because Bridie worked long and late in the bar she didn't have the same affinity with her mother.

According to Pat Gillane, Nonie Gordon knew of his affair with her younger daughter Bridie, but she didn't tell anyone because she didn't want to lose Phil. But after the confrontation in the kitchen over Pat's infidelity, he and Philomena decided to build their own house on a plot of land on his farm at Glenbrack, near Gort, and begin a new life together, away from the temptation of Bridie.

Philomena Gillane was either a very wise and thrifty woman or she had a second source of income that nobody knew about. She wore expensive jewellery, had a 91G car and £196,000 in the bank, a considerable sum. She also paid for much of the building work on the new house – and only the best of everything went into it.

But the money had to come from somewhere. Pat earned a bit as a lorry driver and he helped around the farm, but Philomena was the main earner in the house. That was why, that Wednesday morning, May 11, she was driving down the long avenue towards the main road and Dublin to begin her week-long shift in the kitchens of Loughlinstown hospital.

Later, Nonie Gordon would say she heard a gunshot early that morning. It wasn't such a strange sound in the country and it was only a week later that it would take on enormous significance.

When the family rose that morning there was nothing out of place and they carried on as normal. Because there wasn't a phone in the house they didn't expect to make contact with Philomena until the following Wednesday when she would return home for her week off.

It might seem odd that herself and Pat would have little contact in that time, if only to chat about their young son, but he insisted that the arrangement was that he would phone her at Loughlinstown hospital the following Sunday at 5.30 p.m.

When he did make the call, from Bergin's pub in Mount Bellew, Pat Gillane was told that his wife Philomena had not appeared for work the previous Wednesday and hadn't been seen since. He went back to the bar and ordered another pint and it wasn't until 7 p.m. that he phoned the local gardaí and reported her missing.

The following day, Monday, the gardaí released details of the missing woman and on Tuesday Pat Gillane went on *Morning Ireland*, RTE's early morning radio programme, and made an impassioned plea for anyone who could help in the search for his wife.

'My head is in a daze and I just don't know what to do, but I feel something strange has happened,' he said.

When a version of the interview was played on Shannonside Radio the next day, Pat Heneghan, a car enthusiast who worked for a contract cleaning company, was listening. He mentally noted the registration 91G 3326 as he had with other numbers down through the years. Pulling out of Athlone railway station within minutes of the radio item he noticed a car with that registration parked facing the main road, its rear to the railway track.

He got out and looked at it – and saw the keys still dangling in the ignition. A travel case containing women's clothing, make-up and other personal effects lay open on the front passenger seat and a white plastic sack lay on the floor behind. He went into the station and made a phone call to the gardaí.

Garda Brendan Kerins who was in charge of the crime scene found the car locked but with two of the windows slightly open. The cord of an anorak was dangling from the boot of the hatchback. He organised cutting equipment to get the door opened. When gardaí took the keys from the ignition and opened the boot there was the slight stench of decomposing flesh in the morning air.

The body, that of a woman still partly clad in night attire, had been lying curled up in the boot for almost a week. The blood from a frenzied knife attack and a gunshot wound had congealed on her clothes and dried into the carpet of the car boot. She had been shot in the back with a cartridge and some of the pellets had burst one of her lungs. Then she had been stabbed six times in the back with the jagged blade of a steak knife. She also had a large bruise on her forehead, grazing and cuts on her right hand and her knees. These were the last remains of Philomena Gillane.

But worse was to come when it was established that she had still been alive when she was bundled into the boot of her own car where for twenty minutes she lay in a daze of agony and terror before drowning in her own blood.

It was a terrible way to die, and for the Gordons and the Gillanes it would unleash a nightmare that goes on to this day. In the days that followed, Pat Gillane played the part of the grieving husband but within hours of the funeral simmering tensions between the Gordons and the Gillanes began to surface.

Murder detectives quickly established that Pat Gillane had been having an affair with his wife's sister. They also found out about the row in Bergin's bar the previous Christmas. They could find no motive for anyone else to have murdered Philomena Gillane; the evidence, circumstantial as it was, only pointed in one direction.

Five days after the funeral a long-time neighbour of the Gillanes, John Cahill from Coole Park in Gort, asked Pat Gillane straight out if he had killed his wife.

'No,' he answered.

Cahill then asked him who did he think killed her.

'A crowd from Dublin,' he answered.

'Rumours went around that Pat and I did it,' said Kevin Gillane, Pat's only brother. 'But I had no hand, act or part in the murder of Philomena and neither had Pat.'

But all the talk and the close attention of detectives to Pat Gillane saw the tension mounting in Beechlawn House. And the husband wasn't the only one under suspicion. On May 24 Bridie Gordon was arrested and held for forty-eight hours under Section 30 of the Offences against the State Act. She was questioned about the alleged unlawful possession of firearms. Did gardaí think she was an accomplice in the killing of her own sister, or were they trying to soften her up so that she would admit to her affair and put her lover, Pat Gillane, in the frame? 'I was brought in in the wrong,' she said.

Within days of the funeral Pat Gillane moved out of Beechlawn House and back to live with his brother Kevin. He said Nonie Gordon had hit him over the head with a stick and he had to get six stitches. At a family meeting it was decided that little John Michael should go to live in Oranmore with Pat's sister Martina Riordan and her husband and three children.

A few weeks later Pat Gillane was arrested under the Offences against the State Act. But he didn't answer detectives' questions, 'only the one's that suited him', and there was no evidence to link him directly to his wife's savage murder.

The lapse of a week between the murder and the finding

of the body caused enormous difficulty for detectives in the investigation team – and it gave the murderer time to dispose of vital evidence such as the gun, the knife, clothes and other incriminating items.

Two shotgun cartridges found in the vicinity of the house in Caltra turned out not to have been connected to the shooting of Philomena Gillane. Detectives couldn't find out where the Opel Kadette had been between the Wednesday morning when Phil left home and the following Tuesday night when it was left at Athlone railway station. They were pretty certain it hadn't been there the previous day.

Relations between the two families, which had once been 'mighty' when they celebrated the christening of baby John Michael together, were now poisonous. Within weeks the enmity boiled over into a farmyard fracas that almost led to the death of second member of the Gordon family.

Martin Gordon believed that Pat Gillane and his brother Kevin had murdered his sister. 'They threw her there like a dog,' he said angrily. After long days of tension following the funeral of their sister, he and his brother Paddy called to the Gillanes' house at Glenbrack to have it out with their brother-in-law. According to the Gordons they wanted to talk about their sister's death and ask Pat directly if he was involved. They knocked on the door and waited around the yard and were just leaving when confronted by the Gillane brothers.

Kevin Gillane gave a different version of what happened that day. 'They [the Gordons] hammered on the doors and windows and were shouting "come out ye bastards and bring the gun and the knife with ye"', a reference to the weapons used in the bloody murder of their sister. Martin Gordon, a tall, long-faced man with a quiet voice, given to dressing in black and nicknamed 'The Undertaker', was especially frightening, according to Pat Gillane.

The four men, two brothers on each side, squared up in the farmyard like participants in an old-style cowboy drama. Suddenly all the pent-up fury erupted in the farmyard. Kevin Gillane had a pickaxe handle in one hand and a baseball bat in the other. He swung the weapons wildly but the Gordons quickly disarmed him and began to use the weapons on the Gillanes. Pat Gillane said that Paddy Gordon was beating his brother Kevin while Martin Gordon was hitting him with the baseball bat, shouting, 'You killed my sister'.

As the melee careered across the farmyard Kevin Gillane grabbed a slash hook that was leaning against the wall of the cowshed and swung it with almost deadly accuracy. It left Martin Gordon with a huge gash across his stomach. 'His guts were hanging out,' said a distraught Paddy Gordon after his brother was taken off to hospital critically injured.

The Gordons' hatred now focused on other members of the Gillane family. Martina Riordan said she had no problem with the Gordons visiting John Michael, but on one occasion she heard them telling the infant loudly, 'When you grow up we'll tell you who murdered your mother.'

Then on May 14, 1995, after attending a Mass for the first anniversary of Philomena's death the Gordons, Nonie, Martin, Paddy, Mary and Bridie drove up to Martina Riordan's front door in Oranmore in Philomena's Opel Kadette car.

'They said, "Get out you fucking tinker and look at the car where your brother put our sister's body." I was very upset,' said Martina.

She said they forced their way into her house and began shouting and abusing her. A friend, visiting at the time, had to take the children upstairs.

A year after the murder and with no sign of Pat Gillane breaking, the detectives who had been painstakingly investigating the killing decided to take the investigation in a different direction. They were no longer looking for the killer, they wanted the man who ordered it.

Within days of Philomena Gillane's murder the investigation into her death had taken a strange and dramatic turn many miles from Caltra. Alan Bailey, a detective in the Bridewell Garda Station in Dublin, was a part-time social worker in the day-care centre for homeless men in Whitefriar Street in Dublin. There he got to know a homeless serial offender with a serious drink problem called Christy Bolger.

Around noon on May 20, 1994, Bolger arrived in the station with a strange, almost unbelieveable tale about meeting a man who had asked him to kill his wife. Bolger insisted this was the same man who had been in the papers the day before, photographed at the funeral of his wife in Co Galway. Bailey was sceptical at first, but that afternoon Bolger arrived back in the Bridewell bringing his friend Michael Doyle and a copy of the previous day's *Irish Independent* which carried a picture of a weeping Pat Gillane at his wife's funeral.

On January 30, 1994, Michael Doyle was walking towards James's Street in Dublin with Christy Bolger. A car stopped alongside them and the driver asked for directions to the Royal Hospital Kilmainham. They told him it wasn't far away and pointed him in the right direction. The driver seemed to stall for a moment, as if unsure what to do next, and then drove off.

A few minutes later the car returned. The driver stopped and spoke to the two men again. He didn't seem daunted by their dishevelled appearance. He asked them if they had jobs and they said no. He asked if they lived in the area. They told him they lived in the Back Lane Hostel, a place for homeless men down at Christchurch, nearer the city centre.

Sensing that there might be something in this for themselves the two men asked him for a cigarette. He said he didn't smoke, but he would get them some fags. He told them to get into the car.

They stopped at a shop in Thomas Street and the man went in and bought cigarettes, unconcerned at leaving them alone in his car. After they lit up he asked if they would 'do a job' for him. When they wondered what kind of job it was, he asked if they knew a quiet place where they could talk. They directed him into Basin Lane Flats where he repeated the question. They inquired what it was, thinking he was looking for sex. But he replied, chillingly, that he wanted them to kill someone.

'We asked him who he wanted killed, and he replied "my

wife",' said Christy Bolger. 'We asked him why and he said she was threatening to take everything he had.'

As they were talking, a Garda patrol car circled around, suspicious at a country registered car in the flats. But after a few moments it moved on.

'He said he would pay us a substantial sum of money if we did this for him,' said Christy Bolger.

Doyle said he and Bolger wanted to talk about the offer and they got out of the car. After a few moments Christy Bolger, himself a hardened criminal, went back to the car, but this time he didn't get in. He spoke to the driver through the car window and asked him if he was a homosexual, or if he wanted a woman. The man told them they must have misunderstood. He asked if they would do such a job, or knew anybody who might do it. When they said no, he told them they were no good to him and he drove off.

The two down-and-outs never imagined they would see this big, ruddy-faced countryman again, but a couple of months later Christy Bolger caught a flash on television of a man standing weeping by an open grave. It was an image that sent a shudder of recognition through him. The following day's paper confirmed that it was the same man.

Now, a year later and everything else having failed, it was time to test their story.

On June 30, 1995, Pat Gillane was arrested in Gort and brought to Mill Street Garda station in Galway. That same day Michael Doyle travelled by train from Dublin to Galway where he was met by detectives. They told him to wait in the hallway of the station and nod his head if he saw someone he recognised. When Pat Gillane passed by he said, 'That's him.'

Later he was brought into a room where Pat Gillane was sitting. There were two other people there and Doyle again identified Gillane as the man who had bought himself and Christy cigarettes and propositioned them to 'do a job'. Pat Gillane called Doyle 'a liar' three or four times. But detectives believed his story, and during two fruitless days of questioning they told Gillane this.

'They are only winos from Dublin, they'll do anything for a drink,' he replied contemptuously.

In September, 1996, more than two years after Philomena Gillane was murdered, her husband Pat Gillane stood in the dock in Galway courthouse charged with soliciting Michael Doyle and Christopher Bolger to murder Philomena Gillane.

Before Judge Raymond Groarke, Pat Gillane was asked, 'How say you, guilty or not guilty?' Dressed in a neat dark blue jacket with a plain white shirt, a patterned tie and black trousers the thirty-four-year-old Gillane with his slicked-back hair cut a dashing figure. 'Not guilty, my Lord,' he replied promptly.

Only a few feet from him sat Nonie Gordon, now old and frail, broken by the murder of her favourite daughter and the scandal that it had brought on the once respected Gordon family. She was to be the State's first witness in the sensational trial and sat with her daughters, Bridie and Mary, and her sons, Paddy and Martin.

Then, just as the first juror, a woman, was about to be

sworn in to hear the case, an anguished cry of 'Get a doctor, get a doctor!' cut through the silence of the hushed courtroom.

Nora Gordon had slumped forward in her chair her head rolling to one side after suffering a fatal heart attack. Bridie screamed uncontrollably, 'Mammy, Mammy – she's dying!' as guards and detectives carried the critically ill grandmother from the court.

Tragedy had struck again. Just seven minutes into the trial which was about to lay bare some of the secrets of her daughter's death Nonie Gordon died, without seeing anybody brought to justice for the murder of her beloved Phil.

The trial of Patrick Gillane did not go ahead in Galway that September. His defence team, led by Eamon Leahy SC, pleaded that he could not get a fair trial in Galway and the proceedings were transferred to the Central Criminal Court in Dublin in December, 1997.

The case against Pat Gillane rested on the testimony of the two homeless men. It seemed to descend into farce when Christy Bolger claimed that he had a microchip in his head.

'I know people can read my mind. I had a microchip placed in my skull which is connected to my mouth,' he said in one bizarre passage of evidence.

He admitted that he had forty convictions and was detained 'five or six times' in the Central Mental Hospital in Dundrum. He had just been released from Cork Prison when he saw the picture of Pat Gillane in the paper. The other prosecution witness, Michael Doyle, agreed during the trial that when he first went to the gardaí with Bolger he had confirmed meeting Gillane on a Dublin street, but made no mention of the man saying he wanted his wife killed.

Despite the character of the witnesses, on Wednesday December 8, 1997, more than three and a half years after the murder, a jury of eight women and four men found Pat Gillane guilty of soliciting the two down-and-outs to kill his wife, Philomena. Judge Joseph Matthews sentenced him to eight years in prison for the crime.

Pat Gillane, always immaculately dressed and who had acted like a peacock posing for photographers as he went in and out of court, suddenly found himself alone. None of his family were there for this dramatic moment. He was a man isolated by his past and by the secrets that lay buried in his soul. Deserted by his own kin and detested by the family that had taken him in when he married Philomena, he was truly abandoned by all.

Suddenly he began to weep. As the tears coursed down his rosy cheeks he must have wondered how it had come to this. Once he had a home and a family, the love of two sisters. Now he was facing into eight years in prison on the evidence of the two down-and-outs he had treated so dismissively as winos.

There was no evidence as to how and in what circumstances his wife met such a brutal end. There was no gun, no knife, no time of death, no place of death, no killer, no witnesses and no forensic evidence. In fact there was little or no evidence at all – yet Pat Gillane was going to pay a heavy penalty for the life of his wife.

It should have been the end of the affair, but there was another tragic twist left in this lurid story of sex and violence and the end of innocence for the Gordon family. Four years after these events the name Philomena Gillane was mentioned in connection with an inquest into the suicide of a publican in Mountmellick, Co Laois. Denis Donoher, the owner of the Central Bar shot himself after Mary Gordon, the eldest of the sisters, who had worked in the bar for eighteen years and carried on an affair with him for much of that time, left him after falling for another man. He could no longer bear to be without her and he took his own life.

There really did seem to be some fatal attraction about those Gordon girls.

3

DON'T RUIN YOUR LIFE

As the sun came up that August morning she could tell by the heat haze over Killiney bay that it was going to be a fine hot day, the start of the promised heatwave. She pulled on a sleeveless black top with beige spots from Next and a pair of navy Bermuda shorts.

It was a simple outfit on a beautiful woman. Thirty-two-year-old Patricia O'Toole had long, naturally blonde hair falling in curls around her shoulders and a tanned and well-toned body from working out in the gym. She didn't need fancy clothes or designer labels to make her look good.

She wore a distinctive Russian ring with three bands of differently coloured gold which her husband Brian had bought some years before in a shop on Grafton Street. She also wore her wedding ring. It had only been on her finger for a little over a year now, but how much longer it would remain there was a question she kept asking herself.

It was going to be another long day at the office, but the evening was promising. A girl she worked with was leaving the firm and Patricia and her friends had already planned the send-off around the corner from the office in Scruffy Murphy's pub starting at 5 o'clock.

As she left their home in Watson Avenue, a small housing development in the south Dublin suburb of Killiney, her husband's words were still ringing in her ear.

'If you're going drinking tonight don't bring the car,' Brian O'Toole pleaded with his wife.

She ignored him, of course, driving her neat white Peugeot 205 to Mount Street in the centre of Dublin where she worked as a clerk in the offices of Consolidated Insurance Brokers.

When 5 o'clock struck that Friday, August 30, 1991, people came pouring out of the many offices along Mount Street and by the time Patricia's crowd got to 'Scruffy's' the place was already alive with talk and laughter.

Scruffy Murphy's pub under an archway off Mount Street was a trendy bar before bars had become trendy in Dublin. There was a big square counter in the centre of the pub and Paddy Mulligan, the colourful fun-loving owner, presided over the place greeting a clientele that included politicians, public relations executives, businessmen, newspaper editors, and staff from the insurance companies that lined Mount Street.

Dobbin's Bistro, a famous Dublin restaurant run by another colourful character, Johnny O'Byrne, was around the back, and many of its wealthy patrons came into Scruffy's either before or after having a meal there.

'She was in great form,' Pat Dunne, the manager of Scruffy Murphy's remembered. 'She was always a very happy girl.' A couple of weeks before on a quiet evening Pat and Patricia had put on wide-brimmed hats and dark glasses and entertained the bar with a spontaneous Blues Brothers routine.

Scruffy's was that kind of place and Patricia was that kind of woman, bright, vivacious and always ready for a bit of fun. She was a good-time girl.

This Friday evening the barman teased Patricia about her hair, saying it was dyed when in fact he knew she was a natural blonde. There was the usual banter as she stood at a corner of the bar drinking a pint of Budweiser with Paula, Amanda, Terry, Irene and Kevin. It was normal office chat, spiced up with a little backbiting. People were coming and going to their group and a presentation of a bouquet of flowers was made to Rosemary Burke, who was leaving.

During the evening Patricia danced across the bar-room floor with Alan Devlin, a well-known Dublin actor. He was famous for walking off the stage during a performance of *HMS Pinafore* in the Gaiety Theatre, telling the audience, 'Fuck this for a game of soldiers – I'm going for a pint.'

At around 10 p.m. Patricia, Paula, Amanda and Rosemary left the pub and went up to the Abrakebabra on Baggot Street.

'Did anyone ever have a kebab when they were sober?' one of them joked.

It was turning into another late, drink-fuelled Friday night for Patricia, a typical double-income-no-kids woman. This was the good life. Why would she bother going back to the empty house in Killiney when her husband wouldn't even be at home?

Amanda left after eating the kebab, while Paula and Rosemary piled into Patricia's car and she drove up to Russell's pub in Ranelagh. There they met another another girl from work, Evelyn Cooper and her husband Gary. Shortly after 11 o'clock Patricia, Evelyn and Gary left Russell's and went to O'Brien's pub on the far side of the street.

By now Patricia had been drinking for six hours and she was fairly drunk. Closing time, then 11.30 p.m., came and went and eventually they were the last people in the pub. The bar manager, Frank Lavelle, who knew Evelyn Cooper and her husband, told them it was time to go.

'Its half-twelve,' he said, a little testily.

'Fuck off,' answered Patricia O'Toole, showing a less gentle side to her nature.

'What did you say?' he asked, slightly shocked at the words coming from such a beautiful mouth.

'Get your nostrils cleaned, you heard me,' she answered, enigmatically.

He just walked away and the three of them left shortly afterwards.

They went up the street to The Pronto Grill, a late-night diner frequented by people who wanted another drink or just weren't in the mood for going home. They asked for a bottle of white Piat D'Or wine. The waitress, Patricia Magee, thought they were drunk but she was given the go-ahead to serve them. Gary Cooper had one glass of wine and the two women polished off the bottle.

The Coopers offered to walk Patricia to her car, which was parked further up the road past what is known as The Triangle in Ranelagh. But she said she was going down to Sachs nightclub where her friend Irene Kelly worked on the cash desk. She said goodbye and walked off into the balmy August night.

But Patricia O'Toole wasn't going to Sachs. She had other plans for what was left of the night, and she wasn't letting anybody else in on the secret. If her husband wasn't going to be at home, there was another man in her life she liked to confide in. She hadn't seen him in over a year, but their relationship was like that, they connected when she needed company.

It was just past 1.30 a.m. when the thirty-two-year-old blonde sat into her little Peugeot and set off on her mysterious odyssey.

At about the same time Sean Courtney emerged from a function in the West County Hotel in Chapelizod on the west side of Dublin with a pint of lager in his hand. He'd already drunk between twelve and thirteen pints and the taxi man wouldn't take him and his friends home. So he threw the pint, glass and all, over the wall and the four people squashed into the taxi: Sean and his girlfriend, Rosaleen Holland, and Stephen Stack and Una Madden.

When they got to Devoy Road, Inchicore, where Stephen and Una lived, Sean fell asleep on a sofa while the others watched a video of *Three Men and A Little Lady*.

The film ended and Una and Stephen said they were going

to bed. Rosaleen Holland didn't know her way out of the estate so Stephen Stack got one side of Courtney and she got the other and between them they managed to haul the semi-comatose soldier as far as Hyland's shop on the main road. Their flat was nearby, so Stephen said goodnight and left them there.

Courtney was propped up against the wall of the shop and Rosemary Holland prepared to cajole him the rest of the way to the flat they shared just around the corner.

Leaning against the wall, the demons that tormented Courtney returned as he slowly came to: the touch of a gun barrel at the back of his head, the blood of his friend spattered about the room they once shared in a far-off war zone.

He had grown up a normal lad from a working-class estate in Drimnagh in Dublin. He left school at sixteen and started working with his father as a signwriter. But his childhood dream was to join the army and as soon as he reached the required age of eighteen he signed up. By then, his girlfriend Amanda was pregnant with their first child. They got married the following year.

Army life was 'everything I ever wanted' he recalled, and at Christmas 1986 Private Sean Courtney decided to go to the Lebanon with the Irish peace-keeping mission.

It was a good money-spinner and when he came home after his first tour he and Amanda were able to move from Tallaght to a house in Leighlin Road in Crumlin and fit it out with the proceeds. Six months later with Amanda pregnant with their second child he went back to the Lebanon on a second tour of duty.

But this time things did not go according to plan.

He was stationed in the Arab village of Ittazutt where the Irish peacekeepers had a very good relationship with the local Arabs. They taught them how to play hurling and brought out presents of football jerseys for the kids. In return they were often invited into people's homes for tea or a bite to eat and Sean Courtney was on first name terms with a number of the villagers.

Then, on a hot June night in 1988, an Israeli tank began to shell the village. The locals emerged with AK47s and a rocket launcher.

The Irish peacekeepers tried to intervene but the villagers' mood had turned ugly and, as the Israeli tank retreated into the hills, a full-blown confrontation erupted between the peacekeepers and villagers. One villager put the barrel of a rifle to the back of Private Courtney's head and demanded to be taken to the Irish camp commander.

Order was restored but later that day when an Irish army personnel carrier arrived in the area the jumpy villagers mistook it for another Israeli incursion and fired on it and one of them appeared to be about to throw a grenade. Courtney, who was stationed on the roof of a village house, fired four warning shots. Unfortunately one of the Arabs was hit by a ricochet and crawled into a field, wounded.

The locals felt betrayed and bitter about the incident and said they were going to 'get' the Irishman. He was moved to another post.

Still shaken from the experience, Sean Courtney came home to Ireland in July for the birth of his second child. He drank a lot and got his leave extended. When it was time to return, he flew to Heathrow Airport in London but the events of that day in the Lebanese village came flooding back and he couldn't board the El Al flight to Tel Aviv. He flew back to Dublin instead.

Eventually he did go back to the Lebanon. A couple of days later the soldier with whom he shared a room, Paddy Wright, was celebrating his birthday. Wright was allowed four cans of lager for the celebration. While Courtney was writing a letter on the bed, Paddy Wright went into the toilet carrying his rifle. There was a loud bang and Courtney jumped to open the door. His friend's body fell out on the floor.

'There were bits of him around the toilet,' he said, describing the horrifying scene.

When he came home Courtney was a different person. He was drinking heavily, he had lost interest in his family and he flew into uncontrollable rages.

'I sobbed my heart out to my ma. I couldn't sleep at night and I'd jump in terror at noises like a car backfiring,' he said.

Sean Courtney couldn't wait to get into the army, now he couldn't wait to get out of it. His marriage was falling apart. He was just twenty-four years old when Amanda told him in June, 1989, that she could stand his behaviour no longer, she was leaving him.

'I wasn't upset, I was glad. I couldn't stand them in the house,' he said.

Even in full uniform Courtney was a slight enough figure, small and puny with a black moustache. But he was attractive to women. The following April at a nightclub he met nineteen-year-old Rosaleen Holland and they soon fell in love. He was still drinking heavily but there was an incredible chemistry between them.

She put up with his rages. There had been an incident in Tramore, Co Waterford, when they went away with another couple and he had got into a fight, while just a few weeks before, he and Rosaleen had gone to Westport in Mayo with some friends from the football club and a violent row had erupted outside a chip shop. Courtney threw the chips into a field and then jumped into the car and roared around the countryside by Croagh Patrick at seventy miles an hour. His friend who was sitting in the car when Courtney got behind the wheel said he'd never been more terrified in his life.

Sean Courtney had been hospitalised briefly in a military hospital after his final trip to the Lebanon, but the doctors couldn't find anything wrong with him and he was soon back on active service.

Now, outside Hyland's shop at 4.10 in the morning and he barely able to stand, Rosaleen was preparing to drag Sean on the last stage of their journey when a car pulled up.

'Excuse me, do you know the way to Connolly Avenue?' asked the attractive blonde woman, leaning across the passenger seat to ask directions through the opened window.

Aidan Cullen, an aircraft mechanic, was on his way to start the early shift at Airmotive, an engine maintenance facility on the Naas Road. It was 6.35 a.m. on Saturday morning. Although the roads were quiet at the weekend he was used to this obscure route which took him across the foothills of the Dublin mountains, down into Tallaght and then on to the Naas Road.

As he passed the GAA club on Mount Venus Road he spotted lying by the roadway what he thought at first glance was a tailor's mannequin, the type of thing you see in shop windows.

'When I looked in the rear view mirror I could see it was a body. It was hard to see exactly at a distance, but I knew something was wrong,' he said.

He drove on and met two golfers going for an early morning game. He asked them to watch over the body and he kept going until he reached a phone box, where he called the gardaí.

When detectives got to the scene they found a naked woman, 5'3" in height lying in the gateway of the GAA club. Her clothes were scattered on the ground and her bloodied head had been beaten repeatedly with a brick or a rock, making the woman's face virtually unrecognisable. Her skull was fractured and her nose had been flattened into her face with the flesh from her once full lips torn off. Both her cheekbones were broken and her upper jaw was so badly smashed that it had become completely separated from the base of her skull. Her hands and arms had suffered eleven different injuries and there was bruising on her left thigh and the mouth of her vagina.

There were blood splashes more than nine feet away from the body. Even the battle-hardened investigators were horrified by the scene and the ferocity of the attack on a defenceless woman.

Strangely, there was no identification on the body. All that Saturday detectives waited for someone to call in a missing person report that would identify the battered corpse. Nobody called.

Although a murder hunt was in progress detectives were hampered in the hours after the grisly discovery by not knowing anything about the victim. It was most unusual that an attractive, married woman, if her rings were anything to go by, did not have someone worried about her going missing for an entire night.

At about the time that Aidan Cullen discovered the naked woman's body on the narrow mountain road, Brian O'Toole was about ten miles away, driving through the early morning heat haze towards his home. It was just a few minutes before 7 a.m. when he turned into Watson Avenue in Killiney and an empty house. It was Saturday morning, nobody was stirring, nobody witnessed him get out of his car and quietly enter the house.

Brian and Patricia O'Toole met at a barbeque in 1984. They lived together for four years and got married in 1990 at a quiet registry office ceremony in London. Both led eventful lives before they met. She had worked in Germany after leaving school and then travelled in India and Nepal, following the hippy trail. On the way back she had lived in Greece and had a love affair with an Iranian, who later followed her to Dublin. Brian, a big, good-humoured and gregarious chap who loved the atmosphere of the rugby club bar had lived in Spain for a few years, and been married there.

They were a modern suburban couple who lived in the fast lane. Patricia was determined to do better than her current job as an insurance clerk; she had ideas and ambitions. 'Trish was always taking courses,' according to her friend, Irene Kelly. The latest had been a diploma in fitness from Thomond College. This was what she really wanted and she would tell anyone who would listen that her future was as an aerobics teacher, either in Friarsland, the south Dublin gym where she worked out, or even setting up her own business.

For her thirtieth birthday Brian had given Patricia a sleek black Golf as a present. At the time business was booming, his company Promo Ideas International (Ireland) Limited having done very well out of the World Cup in 1990, running marketing promotions and benefiting from the free-spending Irish public.

But now things weren't so good. The car was gone and Brian O'Toole had an enormous overdraft of £30,000 from National Irish Bank. The bank wanted their money. Brian told them he had interests in Spain and was expecting money from there. Later he stopped answering their letters. When the bank manager called to the company's rented office in Adelaide Road in Dublin's city centre, he was told by the landlord to get in the queue, Brian O'Toole owed him three months rent. The company's secretary had returned from holidays in the Canaries to find the office abandoned and the company no longer trading.

Then the bank discovered that the O'Tooles' house in Watson Avenue was on the market for a quick sale at a price of £75,000. There was a rumour going around that Brian O'Toole was thinking about going to Spain so the bank went to the High Court and got an order against him.

Patricia was against selling the house, especially since it was to pay a business debt. She told Brian to find another way out of his financial difficulties. Their differences over the house and the collapse of the business brought strain and tension into their marriage.

Brian O'Toole found work as a bouncer in Buck Whaley's nightclub in Leeson Street, a melting pot of nightclubs, bad wine and late night sexual activity, that only closes up as dawn breaks over the city. He left the club that Saturday morning with a girl.

When he got home at about 7 a.m. he went to bed. He got up at lunchtime on Saturday and went to play a round of golf with some friends from Seapoint Rugby Club. Returning to Watson Avenue that evening, he changed and headed into Buck Whaley's. Brian O'Toole seemed unconcerned about the whereabouts of his wife.

At about 6 a.m. on the Sunday morning, Brian got home and, with still no sign of Patricia, he fell asleep. It was only later in the day that he rang Cabinteely Garda station to report her missing. He was asked to come down to the station.

Why, detectives immediately wondered, hadn't Brian O'Toole missed his wife for two nights?

As he was interrogated on the whereabouts of his wife, Brian O'Toole asked several times if he could use the phone. He called home, claiming that Patricia might have returned to the house and would come down to the station to sort this out.

But detectives knew with grim certainty that that would never happen: Patricia's sister, Ann Scannell, had been listening to the radio at home that Sunday lunchtime when she heard a description of a woman found in the Dublin mountains.

'I said to Pete, I'm sure that's Patricia, I'm going to ring the guards.'

At 4 p.m. her husband, Peter Scannell, identified the body, lying unclaimed in the City Morgue for nearly thirty-six hours, as Patricia O'Toole of Watson Avenue, Killiney. Also that Sunday afternoon Patricia's car had been found abandoned at Suir Bridge, along the Grand Canal. There were two bloody palm prints on the steering wheel.

The detectives did not tell Brian O'Toole that his wife had been murdered, that her body had already been identified. They wanted to find out what he knew first.

Brian O'Toole was either a bloody good actor or he was guilty as hell, thought one of the detectives sifting through the evidence for some clue as to what happened to Patricia O'Toole.

After four hours the interrogation seemed to be going nowhere, so suddenly one of the detectives dropped the Russian ring on the table. 'Is that Patricia's?' he asked.

Brian said he couldn't be sure, such rings were common enough at the time.

> But when the other ring – our wedding ring – dropped on the table it was as if my whole life ended. I just broke down. It was as simple as that. I said, 'It can't be,' and at that stage they said 'We're very sorry' and they offered me a cup of tea and asked if I wanted to sit down. I still couldn't believe it was hers and maybe the rings could have been stolen . . .

And then the slow realisation dawned on Brian O'Toole that he was suspected of killing his own wife because of the delay in reporting her missing.

What was he hiding?

As the details of his life with Patricia were laid bare, what emerged was a marriage that was troubled and a personal life that was a mess.

Detectives began to piece together Patricia O'Toole's movements after she left her friends at The Triangle in Ranelagh the previous Friday. They were amazed that she hadn't crashed the car or been arrested for drunk driving, given the amount of alcohol she had consumed and her erratic driving.

Instead of heading for Sachs Hotel as she had said, Patricia had driven up to the canal, turned left, and started driving west towards Inchicore. She was going in search of Connolly Avenue, where an old flame, Christopher Hoctor, lived. She occasionally visited his house. Patricia O'Toole needed a shoulder to cry on; she was trying to find comfort from the troubles of the present by delving back into the past.

At Keeper Road she pulled up alongside Patricia Brady and her boyfriend Cormack and asked if they could give her directions to Connolly Avenue. They said they didn't know where it was and she pulled away. Then she stopped and reversed back and asked them if they wanted a lift. They declined.

Paul Barry and Tony O'Brien were standing in the forecourt of Windsor Motors on the South Circular Road when the Peugeot car pulled in beside them. Patricia O'Toole wound down the window.

'Could you tell me the way to Inchicore? I'm going to a party and I've lost my way,' she said.

They gave her directions and she sped off, grinding the gears as she went and taking the wrong road.

At 2.20 a.m. two barmen, Conor O'Leary and John Fitzgerald, were cycling home from work when suddenly at Suir Bridge a car came towards them on the wrong side of the road.

'Will you show me the way to Connolly Avenue?' asked the driver.

'We're going home from work and that's all we can do,' said John Fitzgerald, giving her directions.

Just then a car pulled up and the driver leaned out the window, asking 'What's wrong?'

Patricia O'Toole spoke to him and as the two barmen got back up on their bicycles they heard the driver of the white Fiat 127 tell Patricia in a loud voice, 'Hold on there a minute and I'll get you organised.'

It was 4.10 a.m. when the car pulled up opposite Hyland's shop.

'Excuse me, do you know the way to Connolly Avenue?' she asked.

The man leaning drunkenly against the wall came to life and went over to her. He began to give her directions, but the woman said she didn't understand.

'Could you show me the way?' she pleaded.

'I'll show you if you want, but will you drop my girlfriend off at our flat?' the man answered.

The couple got into the car and Patricia drove about two minutes to the flat.

'Don't be long,' the girlfriend said as she got out of the back seat. She was very tired but didn't seem alarmed that her boyfriend was going off alone with a strange and very attractive woman.

As they drove down the darkened road he told the woman he was glad his girlfriend was safely at home.

'It's late at night – you wouldn't know who would be out,' he remarked to the driver without a trace of irony in his quiet Dublin voice.

They chatted amiably, given the amount of drink they had

both consumed. When she enquired about his girlfriend he said that he was married but separated. She told him she was getting separated herself.

'You probably have a different side to separation than I would – being a girl,' he said. He told her he was in the army.

They came to a junction of five roads with Connolly Avenue straight ahead of them. The car stopped and she put her hand on his leg. They looked at each other.

Suddenly she turned to him. 'I could get you done for attacking me,' she said. 'It would be your word against mine.'

She said it in a serious voice. Then she laughed. But it was too late, something had already snapped inside his fragile brain. Sean Courtney hit Patricia O'Toole straight in the face with his left fist. Shocked, she tried to put her hands up to shield the blows, but she was no match for the well-trained soldier whose fists smashed her face in a flurry of physical brutality. Grunting incoherently he hit her again and again until she slumped unconscious on the steering wheel.

He jumped out of the car. He thought about running away but instead he pulled her across into the passenger seat. Then he went around and sat into the driver's seat and gunned the car up the road.

He drove fast, crying to himself and rocking back and forth. The woman made no sound and gradually he left the suburbs behind and started into the foothills of the Dublin mountains. He remembered passing The Creek pitch and putt club, because he had played there once, years before.

Suddenly he asked himself: 'What am I doing?'

He stopped the car and began to turn around on the narrow road to go back to the city. As he did so the woman regained consciousness. Her face covered in blood, she began to scream. He started to scream too.

'I told her she was all right. We were going back to the city and not to worry,' he claimed.

But she kept screaming.

Suddenly she got the passenger door open and tried to get out. He grabbed her. There was a confusion of blows as he tried to hold on to her and she fought for her life. Then he lost his grip and she flopped out of the open door and onto the sandy ground at the entrance to the GAA club where the car had come to a halt.

> I went out the passenger door after her. She was going backwards along the ground, moving on her back, propelling herself on her hands and legs. She was still screaming. I was in a panic. The rock was on the ground. I just picked it up. I didn't mean to kill her . . . I'm sorry.

He hit her with the brick, and he kept hitting her. He cannot remember how many times he hit her, but by the time he finished, her head was a bloody pulp and her face a ruin.

Then he heard her say in a weak voice, 'Don't ruin your life.' Sean Courtney dropped the brick.

As Patricia O'Toole lay dying on the ground Courtney ripped off her clothes scattering the flimsy garments around on the sandy ground.

> I couldn't remember her face. I just can't see it.
> It's like I was standing away from it. I wasn't
> there. I was looking down at it. I just seen the
> girl lying there. She just stopped breathing. The
> sound was so quiet at that time of the morning.
> I just felt sick.

He got back into her car and tried to reverse. He was in a state of panic and shock. Eventually he got into gear and the car shot backwards and he felt a bump. It was the car running over the body, but he didn't know it at the time.

He stopped the car on Dolphin Road near Suir Bridge and got out. He was covered in Patricia O'Toole's blood. It was on his hands and up his arms and on his face and his clothes.

> I looked at my hands, they were red with blood.
> A police car went by and as it did I threw the
> keys into the canal and walked up Suir Road

He stopped by the canal and washed the blood from his hands and then walked back to the flat. It was now between 8 a.m. and 9 a.m. on Saturday morning.

He had no keys so he rang the bell. Nobody answered. He began throwing change from his pockets at the upstairs window. Then he saw the frosty face of his lover at the window. Rosaleen Holland came down and answered the door. She didn't look at him or speak to him. She turned and went back upstairs and got into bed. He undressed in the room and got into bed too. He put his arms around her.

I just wanted to hold somebody. I just couldn't
understand why I had killed the girl, or why
what had happened, happened.

Rosaleen told him he was freezing and to get away from her.

Later that Saturday he got up and washed his clothes in the
washing machine. Rosaleen remembered this later because
the dye from his trousers ran and the clothes all came out
tinged blue.

As the days wore on he felt sick and disturbed. It was like
something out of a Hitchcock film. He had murdered a
complete stranger for no apparent reason.

But was there a reason, something Patricia O'Toole had
said in the car that set off the murderous rage?

Sean Courtney even tried ringing the incident room in
Tallaght, the centre of the investigation, but the phone was
engaged and he never got through.

Only one person, Rosaleen Holland, knew of Sean
Courtney's missing hours on the night of the murder. She told
nobody.

Although detectives were beginning to close in they were
still trawling through the owners of more than 2,350 Fiat 127
cars in the mistaken belief that the driver of one of them had
been the last person to see Patricia O'Toole alive.

Nine days after the murder Courtney collected Rosaleen
Holland and a friend, Elizabeth Abbey, from work in his
Escort car. It was 3 p.m. Monday September 9, 1991. The car
radio was on and the newsreader said that gardaí believed

Patricia O'Toole had given two people a lift the night she was murdered. Sean Courtney snapped off the radio.

He dropped the other girl home and drove back to the flat. He said to Rosaleen he had something to tell her and asked her to go back out to the car and get a copy of the *Evening Herald* from under the seat, but not to look at it. When she did so, he took it from her and unfolded it. There was a picture of Patricia O'Toole on the front page.

'I just kept looking at the picture, I couldn't believe what he was saying to me, that he'd killed the girl,' she said. She recognised the woman as the driver of the car who had asked for directions.

They hugged each other. Then he told her he had to go back to work in Cathal Brugha Barracks. He rang her again at 6.50 p.m. that day and told her not to worry, that he would do the worrying.

But later that night she rang some friends, and almost immediately they descended on the flat and took her away to Ballyfermot, where she was from originally.

The following day, Tuesday, at 12.45 p.m. Sean Courtney was arrested at the barracks by a group of detectives.

At the trial of Sean Courtney in Dublin in January, 1993, Paddy McEntee SC, the country's best-known criminal barrister, painted a picture of an Irish soldier deeply traumatised by his tours of duty with the Irish peace-keeping missions to Lebanon. He was, said Mr McEntee, suffering from a disorder called post-traumatic stress disorder as a result of a number of incidents, including the day his friend shot himself.

'I was like a grenade with the pin off, waiting to explode,' said Sean Courtney.

In an interview he gave the morning he was due to be sentenced, he said he had 'never hit a woman in my life' until that fatal night he took a lift from Patricia O'Toole. 'I always thought killers were people foaming at the mouth, but it's not like that,' he said.

But Sean Courtney never fully revealed what happened in Patricia O'Toole's car that fatal August morning.

Seconds after he was sentenced to life in prison for the murder of Patricia O'Toole, the ugly side of the soldier reappeared when he roared above the bustle of the empyting courtroom, 'She was only a fucking tramp.'

Was that the real reason for the savage attack? Did Patricia O'Toole mock his manhood because he 'couldn't get it up' as they sat together in the car as dawn broke over Dublin?

Only Sean Courtney knows the truth and he's still in jail.

4

THE BLACK MASK

She teased him gently with the prospect of languid hours of exotic sex. Her promises were so provocative he couldn't stop thinking about them every moment of the hours and days that followed.

Their affair was over, he had promised his wife. He didn't want to start it all over again; getting involved with her filled his life with unwanted complications. But the desire that burned for her had never really gone away. Now he couldn't resist the lure and the promise.

Apart from the sex, it would take his mind off more pressing problems. He was in a dangerous business. His young associate, whom he'd brought into the firm and taught everything he knew, had turned on him. First he had wanted a slice of the action and when he got that, he wanted more.

Then there were the shadowy figures that hung around the border towns where he did his business. They claimed to be the IRA. Who knew? But they were dangerous. He'd kept them at bay with back-handers and promises of more to come. But they were getting greedier with each passing day. With the ceasefire they had nothing else to occupy themselves apart from the odd punishment beating and prying into other people's business.

As he walked the streets or drove along the narrow roads he could almost feel their eyes burning into his back. He had been around long enough to know that all it took was one wrong word or a false move and he would end up lying in a ditch by the side of the road with a bullet in the back of his head.

The police on both sides of the border were also investigating his affairs – his financial ones, that is. That too was a cause for concern but he could deal with it. For a decade now he'd been able to stay one step ahead of the law. He knew the way their minds worked: slow and ponderous. He was fast and agile, flitting from one side of the border to the other, or over to England or the continent when the need arose.

But he wanted to get away from this grown-up game of hide-and-go-seek. He was getting too old for it. He was tired looking over his shoulder all the time in case his enemies were following him. Or, worse still, in case his wife might find out that his passionate affair was still smouldering.

He had promised her solemnly that he was giving up the girl. That was what was holding their marriage together. They had talked about it and decided they would take the children and start a new life where nobody knew them, where nobody would find them. Miami sounded good to him. He had property and investments there and it was just a question of converting his assets into enough cash to start a new life in America.

But in the meantime his mistress just wouldn't stop calling.

In a kittenish voice she painted erotic pictures of passion and indescribable pleasure. They would start in the morning after she came home from Mass. She would lead him to her girly bed with its white, frilly cushions and fluffy soft toys. But the sex would be raw and erotic. She promised it would be.

Paddy Farrell was full of good intentions, but he just wasn't very good at carrying them out. The mixture of the sacred and the profane finally hooked him.

One last time, he promised himself.

Paddy was not an easy man to lure. He was forty-nine now, with a narrow face, bright smiling eyes, a high, wide forehead and carefully dyed dark, receding hair. Dressed in a white shirt, a colourful tie and an expensive suit he looked slim and every inch the prosperous businessman. The sleek car completed the image. He always carried a black briefcase with him and according to associates he kept it well stocked with cash, as much as £70,000 at any given time. His was a cash business.

On the surface he was a prosperous car dealer and pillar of the community who lived with his wife, Anne, and their three children in a big South Fork style house outside Newry, Co Down. He drove an £80,000 E-series maroon Mercedes and there were always a few expensive looking BMW or Mercedes cars parked outside in the grounds. Originally from Culloville, Co Armagh, he'd been living in Newry since 1993. He ran a car dealership in nearby Warrenpoint.

Paddy Farrell was a quiet man who kept a low profile. But in a small place a man gets noticed when he's doing well. He was doing very well and neighbours noted that when there was a collection for the unfortunate children of Chernobyl, Paddy dropped a wad of crisp £50 notes into the collection box.

But Paddy Farrell had a secret life. The car dealership which was doing so well was a cover for a huge cross-border drugs distribution business. The man in the maroon Mercedes was one of the biggest dope dealers in the country with connections stretching to Amsterdam, London and Miami.

He had a string of convictions in England going back to the mid-1960s when he saw the inside of a few cells for house-breaking, car stealing and fighting with the police. As he got older and wiser he turned his hand to social security fraud and ringing cars – stealing top-class motors and fixing them up with false number plates and papers and selling them on. But that was before he broke into the big time.

Like a lot of smart petty criminals he built up a network of contacts – particularly with the Irish boys – and by the 1990s he was making quite a name for himself in the highly lucrative cigarette smuggling business. There was a fortune to be made on the streets of Dublin, Belfast and other cities selling smuggled fags through a network of street sellers.

The drugs business wasn't such a big step up the ladder. He travelled to Liverpool and Amsterdam and he met up with John Traynor, the Irish criminal known as one of the kingpins of the tobacco and drugs trade.

Farrell wasn't long getting himself a slice of the action. But he had his eyes on bigger things. Through Traynor he got an introduction to John Gilligan, the main cannabis distributor in Ireland. Gilligan was then keeping a low profile and making so much money that he employed two people full time just to count it and put it into bundles to be laundered. They were soon doing business together and Paddy Farrell moved back to Ireland with his family, building himself the big house in Newry.

His drugs consignments sometimes contained handguns and ammunition. How he got that stuff into the country interested the IRA, and it also interested the police. The Irish Drug Squad set up a sting called Operation Madonna to try to trap him. Farrell lost a consignment of cannabis worth £500,000 when it was intercepted in Wexford, along with twenty handguns. But Paddy Farrell wasn't compromised, the detectives weren't able to connect him to the operation.

Every dope dealer has to have his mistress and soon after arriving back in Ireland Paddy was infatuated with a beautiful Drogheda girl with the same surname as himself. Lorraine Farrell and Paddy Farrell were not related, they just shared a taste for good living, nightclubs and the sound of champagne corks popping.

She was in her mid-twenties when they met in a nightclub in Newry where she used to socialise with her two sisters. A gorgeous girl with big sparkling eyes, a wide smile that showed her perfect teeth and a fabulous figure, she was slightly mixed up and desperately seeking love. 'She wanted to marry me, and I hardly knew her,' said one of the group of people who hung around the pubs and clubs in Drogheda, Dundalk and Newry.

Lorraine was vivacious, without being over the top and she was a perfect foil for the reserved older man. The smooth-talking car salesman and the beautiful girl with marriage on her mind were lovers within weeks, although Lorraine still insisted on going to Mass every morning. She was a traditional girl in that sense; she believed in redemption.

How much she actually knew about his real business is hard to know. If she knew anything she kept it to herself. But if she knew nothing then she was even more innocent than many of her friends believed. But the border has always been a great place for making money and most people turn a blind eye to what goes on, whether it's smuggling, washing diesel or dealing in dodgy cargoes of one sort or another.

Lorraine's parents, Kieran and Peg Farrell, were separated. When Paddy Farrell first met Lorraine she was living at home with her mother in a small house in Boyle O'Reilly Terrace in Drogheda. Her sister Edel and her mother's partner, Dessie Wilton, also lived there. Peg and Dessie ran a taxi-cab business in the town.

Paddy Farrell was a generous man, especially when it came to someone as special as Lorraine. He soon bought her a house in an estate in Newry just a short distance from his own more impressive home and his wife and children. He gave her money and jewellery, bought her a car and got her a job with a business associate. For Paddy and Lorraine life seemed to be a bed of roses.

But Lorraine wanted something more than that. She wanted to be Mrs Paddy Farrell but after three years together the realisation dawned on her that this was never going to be.

Paddy Farrell was now in the big time. With the money pouring in from the drug trade he was able to launder it and buy property around Newry, in Belfast and London as well as a couple of apartments in the upmarket new development in The Sweepstakes in Dublin 4. He also looked overseas, buying apartments in Miami and Geneva.

But with the murder in 1996 of journalist Veronica Guerin, who had accused drug dealer John Gilligan of a vicious assault, the drug lords were suddenly under pressure. Police on both sides of the border were coming down heavily on the tobacco and cannabis suppliers. New money-laundering legislation was introduced making it harder to get rid of cash. Paddy Farrell was beginning to feel the heat.

There was a greater threat from nearer home, however. The IRA sensed the public mood and drug dealers were getting ultimatums to leave town or have their kneecaps blown off. After one of his associates was ordered out of Newry, Paddy Farrell felt increasingly that the Godfathers of Terror were turning their beady eyes in his direction. They had a huge intelligence-gathering network and his cross-border activities were causing them annoyance and concern.

Paddy Farrell had personal problems too. Some of his associates weren't happy having his mistress living in the same small town as his family. It caused a lot of talk and unnecessary gossip. One night Lorraine Farrell's hall door got daubed with paint and graffiti. There was talk around Newry that it was inspired by the IRA and was a message to Paddy Farrell that they were watching his every move. But others believed the graffiti incident originated closer to home and was really a message to Lorraine that it was time to end the affair and leave town.

She was certainly spooked and moved back across the border to her mother in Drogheda after renting out her house in Newry.

There was a lot of tension in the Farrell household around this time, and during the Christmas of 1996 Paddy Farrell talked out his problems with his wife, Anne, and it was then that they decided to move to Miami with their children, John, Patrick and Charlotte.

But there was always something to be tidied up. By the following September Farrell was still talking of moving, but so far he hadn't gone anywhere. He was only seeing Lorraine very occasionally, wary of the roads between Newry and Drogheda where terrorists lurked and could strike at any time. He was a marked man and he was keeping very much to himself.

Lorraine was pining for him. She had lost about one and a half stone in the nine months since their relationship had cooled. That was when she started calling him again with promises of a day he would never forget.

When he could resist no longer they agreed to a rendezvous in Drogheda at her mother's house on Wednesday morning, September 10, 1997. She would have the house to herself for the day. It would be discreet.

Lorraine Farrell began to prepare for the encounter. That week she bought several pairs of new white panties. She bought thigh-high, black leather boots. She bought a skimpy black PVC lace-up mini-dress. And she bought a mask.

Driving down from Newry that Wednesday, Paddy Farrell's nerves were on edge. He was now practically on the run from the IRA, the shadowy figures he couldn't even see.

He had already called Lorraine on his mobile phone as the big Mercedes car pulled up on the pathway outside her mother's house at around 11 a.m. The car, worth nearly as much as the house, almost seemed to dwarf the small terrace of houses. A neighbour was cutting the lawn. It was a normal Wednesday morning in the suburbs of Drogheda as Paddy Farrell got out and walked the short distance to the front door.

Dressed in blue jeans and a denim top Lorraine opened the door of the otherwise empty house to her lover. They went upstairs almost immediately. She stripped off and changed into the PVC mini-dress and the long leather boots and they began to make love. As he lay on the bed she performed a striptease for him, slowly taking off the boots, the tight-fitting mini-dress and the knickers until she was dressed only in a bra.

He was mesmerised as she started to fulfil the promises she had whispered to him down the phone.

Lorraine handed him the black mask and told him to put it on and lie back on the bed and wait. He did as he was told, lying there on her girlish single bed, his mind and body consumed with the expectation of what was to come.

For a few hours this would wipe away the fears he had for his life. But little did he know that his killer was not some hooded figure in a combat jacket hiding by the side of the road.

His killer was already right there in the room with him.

What Paddy Farrell didn't know was that Lorraine had a second shopping list, and this one was lethal. She had assembled it just as thoroughly as she had assembled the sexy outfit that she had just disgarded.

A friend had told her that a local man was selling a double-barrel shotgun. Lorraine said she had a friend who might be interested and asked if she could see the gun. Her stepfather had driven her out to the house on the other side of town on the previous Sunday, September 7. She examined it carefully, although she knew nothing about guns, and agreed to buy it.

She also called to a neighbour, Paddy Townley, an undertaker who lived down the terrace from her mother's house. She told him she wanted to buy a grave in St Peter's Cemetery in Drogheda. He took her there that day and the gravedigger showed her a plot near her grandmother's, telling her it would cost £200.

That evening the owner of the shotgun arrived at her home in Boyle O'Reilly Terrace with the gun wrapped in a blanket. She paid him £200 in cash and he gave her the gun. After he left she called down to Paddy Townley and paid for the grave. As she stood in the kitchen talking to Townley's wife, she asked about embalming and the process by which it was done.

'When Lorraine told me she'd bought the grave I felt it was a bit morbid. Not strange, but morbid,' said Dessie Wilton.

For some reason it didn't seem strange that she had also bought a shotgun – even if she said it was for somebody else.

Lorraine Farrell was twenty-nine years of age, young, single and outwardly normal. She had her whole life stretching before her. But as she looked at her lover spread-eagled on the bed Lorraine was in a far from normal state of mind.

Lying there with the mask on, it wasn't the soft body of his beautiful lover that touched Paddy Farrell. A sudden thunderous explosion filled the small bedroom as both barrels of the shotgun blasted him between his eye and his ear. The shattering impact blew the top of his head off above the eyebrows. Bits of flesh and bone and fragments of skull were splattered around the room.

The neighbour's lawnmower droned on in the distance, drowning out the sounds from inside the death room.

Lorraine Farrell, who had hardly said an angry word in her life, stood with the smoking gun cradled in her arms, the smell of the shotgun blast still pungent in the air.

She reloaded the gun and fired two shots into the ceiling. The bullets may have been intended for herself, but she just hadn't the courage at that moment to carry out the final act.

Maybe it was the sight of her lover's brains all over the pink-tinted room that tipped the scales. She retreated across the room, reloaded the gun again and, standing just inside the door, fired a third blast. She fell behind the door, almost naked, straddling the barrel of the gun.

The lovers were now together, forever frozen in that moment of death and destruction.

That evening Ireland were playing Lithuania in a soccer international and Peg Farrell and Dessie Wilton came home from the taxi company, passed the Mercedes parked on the path and turned on the television to watch the match.

They didn't know Paddy Farrell very well. 'I only met him a few times and I found him an absolute gentleman,' Peg Farrell recalled.

As the game progressed they could hear mobile phones ringing endlessly in the bedroom above. At half time Dessie Wilton went upstairs, opened the door and looked into the room. He saw the outline of Paddy Farrell lying on the bed, so he closed the door and went downstairs to see the second half of the game.

But one thing struck him as odd. There was no sign of Lorraine's purse. She always left it on the table in the sitting room, or somewhere handy where she could see it. Peg helped him to look for it and found it on the floor, open with a handwritten note sticking out. She picked it up and took out the note which was in Lorraine's handwriting. It was addressed to Peg's other daughter, Edel. As Peg unfolded it, a sum of money fluttered out and fell onto the floor. With mounting horror she read:

Dear Edel,

I want you to have all my jewellery and wear it.
You will enjoy it. There is money also, make use
of it. Thanks for everything. I love you always.
Lorraine

There was a postscript – Lorraine Farrell ordered that white lilies should be the only flowers allowed on her grave.

Dessie Wilton glanced at the letter as Peg Farrell tried to take in its contents. He ran up the stairs two at a time. When he turned on the light in the bedroom he was confronted with the carnage. Ballistics expert Detective Willie Brennan told the inquest that followed:

The pillow underneath Paddy Farrell's head was covered in both blood and brain tissue, while there were two large pieces of skull bone lying inside the door of the room. There were fragments of brain tissue on the footlocker at the end of the bed.

Dessie blocked Peg from coming into the room and slammed the door closed. He then ran down the street to the house of Paddy Townley, the undertaker who had sold Lorraine her grave just days before. It was around 9 p.m. When Paddy Townley touched Lorraine's body he found it cold, with rigor mortis already well set it.

Paddy Farrell had a large sum of English and Irish currency in the pockets of his trousers, which lay crumpled at the end of the bed. In the other upstairs bedroom there was £1,040 wrapped in the bed clothes, and under the bed a bag with twelve shotgun cartridges. In a locker in Lorraine's room there was a powerful stun gun.

The deaths of Paddy Farrell and Lorraine Farrell shocked the town of Drogheda. But the drama wasn't over yet.

Where was Paddy Farrell's briefcase, his associates wanted to know. He always carried it with him. They were not so much concerned with the large amount of cash it would have contained, but they were very interested in papers and documents which might incriminate them, it seemed.

But the briefcase had disappeared.

Paddy Farrell's body was taken back across the border to Newry after the autopsy. While the families of the two lovers grieved, others sought to wreak revenge for what happened in the upstairs bedroom of the small terraced house.

On Friday, September 12, two days after the killings, a Vauxhall Nova car was driven into the town of Drogheda and parked across the entrance to Stockwell Lane just across the street from the taxi-cab company run by Peg Farrell and Dessie Wilton. People walked by the Northern registered car oblivious to what was inside. But the white car they hardly noticed was a deadly time bomb. Someone was intent on more carnage and they didn't particularly care who got killed or maimed in the process.

A crude but deadly copper bomb device had been left inside the car and three barrels of petrol had been strapped together in the backseat. The bomb detonated shortly after noon but instead of shooting backwards and setting off a tremendous explosion when it hit the drums of petrol as had been planned, it went forward, shattered the windscreen of the car and harmlessly lodged in the radiator of a car parked in front of it.

At Lorraine Farrell's funeral her coffin stood in the church surrounded by white lilies, just as she had ordered. Her sisters Edel and Wendy carried gifts that symbolised her life up to the altar: a book on the life of Elvis Presley, her sunglasses and her photograph. Afterwards she was buried in the plot she had so carefully chosen in the days leading up to the double killing.

Across the border in Newry black-clad bodyguards accompanied two limousines carrying Anne Farrell and her family as they escorted the last remains of Paddy Farrell to his grave. The air was tense and heavy with accusation. Lurid stories of the affair etched the grief of the family.

After the funeral a local solicitor issued a statement saying that up to his untimely death Paddy Farrell 'resided with his wife and family and enjoyed a happy and stable marital relationship.'

5

THE ITALIAN JOB

It was after 2 a.m. when the girls got home that Thursday morning. They had just finished a long night's work and they should have been worn out. But they weren't even remotely tired. Tonight was the night they had discussed and dreamed about.

It was the night he died.

The glamorous blonde housewife and the teenage girl, her best friend, went into the kitchen together. They had been laughing a lot but now the joke was over.

The wife reached for a bottle of Italian brandy and poured two glasses. They didn't sip, but drank them greedily as if they would find courage for the deed ahead in the strong amber liquid.

They whispered and hugged each other.

'Are you going to do it?' the woman asked the girl.

'Yes,' she replied.

They had a strange relationship. The elder of the two was just twenty, but she was already married and had more experience of life than many women twice her age. Her fifteen-year-old friend was a local tearaway who had been expelled from school. She began hanging around the takeaway which the woman and her husband operated in a suburban Dublin village. Eventually she was hanging around so much that they gave her a job.

The girls had been best friends for a couple of years and, if anything, their friendship had become so close it was now bordering on a dangerous obsession. Within a few months of her friend's marriage the teenager ran away from home altogether and moved into the newly wed couple's suburban home in leafy Templeogue.

The two girls hugged each other a lot and held hands. The wife showered the young girl with gifts of money, clothes and jewellery. It was a strange ménage à trois. Instead of the wife having to share her husband, it was he who was cuckolded – by an attractive fifteen-year-old girl.

The husband didn't like her. He could smell trouble. A few years behind the counter in a chip shop at two in the morning does that to a person. He told his wife the girl was 'a whore' and 'a slut' and he was going to throw her out of the house.

But she pleaded with him to let the girl stay in their spare room. It wouldn't interfere with his sex life, she assured him. Reluctantly he agreed. But the girl seemed to have a more loving relationship with his young wife than he did and he resented her because of it.

Their whispered conversation over, the girls left the kitchen and went into the living room. The couple, Anna Maria and Franco Sacco, hadn't been living in the house very long and, apart from the big television, it was sparsely furnished, with just a sofa and an armchair.

The handsome husband was stretched out on the sofa, so Anna Maria and the girl sat together on the armchair. He was watching a video of the film *Heat*, a thriller with Robert de Niro and Al Pacino as deadly rivals blurring the edges of good and evil.

On the screen they saw de Niro, playing a gangster, load his gun. The bullets looked like the cartridges her husband used in his hunting rifle. He mostly worked late in their fast food restauraunt, but when he had time his passions in life, apart from sex, were football and hunting.

'You couldn't kill someone with those, they're for hunting,' the wife said innocently, as if butter wouldn't melt in her mouth.

'Fucking sure you could,' he answered and went back to watching the tense drama unfolding on the screen.

As he sat there, a big, tall twenty-nine-year-old stud, with nothing much going on in his head, little did he realise that a real life-and-death drama was unfolding under the roof of his own house.

The girls went back into the kitchen and continued whispering and planning over another glass of brandy. They were still there when the film ended. They heard Franco get up from the sofa and call out 'good night' as he climbed the stairs to bed.

In the kitchen the two girls embraced.

'Do you love me? Am I your best friend?' asked Anna Maria, looking and feeling older than her twenty short years.

'Yeah,' answered the teenager. 'Do you love me?'

'Yeah.'

They held each other tightly.

The girl went to the utility room and came back into the kitchen clasping Franco's hunting rifle in both hands. She was small and petite and the gun looked enormous in her arms.

'Are you going to do it now?' Anna Maria asked.

'Yeah,' said the girl.

Anna Maria went upstairs but came back down quickly and told the girl that her husband was still awake in their bedroom. The girl took the gun and went quietly upstairs and stole into her own room. They had loaded the gun earlier. Now she put it carefully under the bed. She got into the bed but even though it was now very late she couldn't sleep. She lay there thinking about the deed she had offered to carry out for her very best friend. She didn't know anything about guns; she had test-fired the rifle just once and the click of the hammer going down seemed to echo in her head in the quiet of the early morning.

In the next room the young wife got into bed with her husband. For a few moments she blotted out the things that had been happening around her all night, the talk of the killing, the plans to dispose of the body, the offers from friends to help with the deadly plot.

Her husband was wearing just a vest, and around his neck a gold chain. When she got into bed he turned to her and put his hand over her firm breast. He peeled off her T-shirt and knickers greedily. They had sex. He was Italian. He expected it. As he straddled her she could picture the gun going off.

It was over quickly and he rolled away to his own side of the bed and fell asleep. Soon she too fell asleep.

She had set the alarm clock for 9 a.m. but when it went off she re-set it for 11 a.m. and went back to sleep. When she got up her husband also woke.

'Make sure to open the shop on time,' he ordered. He turned over and went back to sleep, his face burrowed into the pillow.

She went into the girl's room and woke her up. The barrel of the shotgun was poking out from under the bed. The girl dressed and they left the room together.

Moments later a gunshot echoed around the walls of the suburban house.

The other young couples living in the estate were gone to work since early morning. Nobody heard the sound of the gunshot, nobody saw the girls leave.

It was the beginning of a very long day and the beginning of the end of their beautiful friendship.

Franco Sacco got his first real kiss from his pert blonde cousin Anna Maria Sacco when she put her tongue in his mouth as a twenty-first birthday present. She was thirteen years of age. They were first cousins once removed and from the sprawling Italian community in Ireland which has run chip shops since the early part of the twentieth century.

Anna Maria's father, Luigi Sacco, had a chip shop in Parnell Street in the centre of Dublin and he lived over it with his Irish born wife Orna, from Donegal, and their daughters

Caterina, Anna Maria, Giovanna and Louisa. Luigi also had a stepson, Danny. Although he lived and worked in Dublin, Luigi, like most of his fellow chip-shop owners, kept a second home in Italy to which he intended to retire.

In 1986 Luigi Sacco wanted to expand his business. He waited until his annual summer holiday in the Italian town of Cassino, south of Rome, from where he originally came, to recruit young men and women who wanted to make their fortune in far-off Ireland.

During that visit he called as usual to see his Uncle Pasquale in the nearby town of Casa Lattico. Luigi told his uncle of his plans to expand his Irish operation. Pasquale said his young son Franco, then eighteen, was a good lad and a good worker and wanted to improve his prospects. Luigi said Franco could make plenty of money working in Dublin. The hours were long, but if he worked hard and showed a bit of initiative he was sure to do well for himself.

Moving to Ireland was a big step for Franco who came from a relatively poor background compared with his Irish cousins. But it was an opportunity he was glad to take. He could see a brighter future working in Ireland than staying at home in his native Italian village.

After a time in Parnell Street the Sacco family moved to a house in Kimmage and Franco went with them. Luigi Sacco opened shops in the satellite Dublin villages of Ranelagh, Rathfarnham and Crumlin.

While Luigi was busy taking care of his new business ventures his earthy young cousin Franco was just as busy taking care of his young daughter Anna Maria.

The Saccos were a big extended family. They all lived in the same house and they all pitched in, working in the family business together. At breaktime in the long sweaty nights over the deep-fat fryer, Franco and Anna Maria began to conduct their passionate love affair.

It wasn't long before the young Irish-born girl was creeping into the bedroom of her hot-blooded Italian cousin for torrid nights of sex. Franco often worked late and the house would be quiet when he got home, until sexy Anna Maria came tapping on his bedroom door.

Luigi Sacco didn't approve of his young daughter's love affair.

'I always had problems with my girls; they wanted to look older than they were,' he said ruefully.

Anna Maria, not only wanted to look older, she wanted to act older, and she was making a very good job of it.

In 1994 the lovers were separated when Luigi took his family to his village in Italy for several months, leaving Franco back in Dublin looking after the shop.

Anna Maria, now eighteen, was beautiful, saucy and proud. She was also more mature than many of the Italian girls her age back in her father's village and was soon a big hit, switching easily from her Dublin English to fluent Italian. Her father was pleased when she took up with a 'respectable' young man he had invited over for coffee.

But the idyllic Italian summer couldn't last forever. Back in Ireland after the sojourn, Anna Maria and Franco took up where they left off. They were from different social and cultural backgrounds and Luigi, doing well from his Irish businesses, had hoped his daughter would make a better match than marrying one of his employees.

But that wasn't to be. Headstrong and proud, Anna Maria had her mind made up. The couple got engaged and planned to marry on her nineteenth birthday.

In preparation, Luigi set up his daughter and future son-in-law in their own chip shop in Rathfarnham, Dublin. They rented it from him for £500 a month and they were beginning to find their feet. But running his own business took its toll and took up a lot more of his time than Franco expected. He had to work longer hours to make the rent money and he didn't have much time to devote to his attractive young fiancée.

Anna Maria had no illusions about life with Franco. He was a typical Italian male chauvinist. He was the boss and what he said went. Not long after their relationship began Anna Maria discovered that Franco had his 'rules' and if she didn't conform the consequences could be ugly.

He had started 'laying down the law' when she was sixteen and from then on he expected to be obeyed. At first he kept her in line with a few 'slaps'.

'If I didn't obey him I got an odd punch or a kick in the legs,' she told her young friend.

This went on until a week before her marriage.

But Anna Maria had found a soul companion to take her mind off her turbulent relationship with Franco. She had become friendly with the young teenager who had already been expelled from school and who acted a lot older than her age.

The two, one on the brink of marriage, the other not much more than a child, became inseparable, going swimming, dancing and doing almost everything together. It was a strange, almost bizarre relationship and from the very start Franco disliked the girl he sometimes called 'that *putana*' – the Italian word for prostitute.

A few weeks before her wedding, as if to assert her independence, Anna Maria and the girl ran away to Edinburgh in Scotland. It was a gesture of rebellion aimed at getting Franco back into line, but there was also something deeper between the two girls from which Franco felt excluded. They stayed there for several days and it was only when Luigi eventually tracked them down and he and Franco pleaded with his daughter to come home, that the two of them returned to Dublin.

'I wanted to give him a fright and get him to stop hitting me,' Anna Maria explained.

On her nineteenth birthday, May 25, 1995, Anna Maria Sacco married Franco Sacco at a lavish wedding banquet in the Victor Hotel in Dun Laoghaire, attended by all the family friends from the Italian community in Ireland. The couple moved into a house in The Glen, off Boden Park in Rathfarnham near the chip shop they were now running together. After some time they moved on, paying £125,000 – a considerable sum at the time – for a new house in

Coolamber Park in Templeogue.

But the marriage never really worked. Anna Maria and Franco were not a happy couple. He was tortured by her relationship with the girl who seemed to get the love he was denied. She lived in mortal fear of her violent husband.

'He left me alone for a good few months when we got married, but it was still mental torture,' she said about the beatings.

Hardly had she arrived home from the honeymoon in Italy but Anna Maria realised she had made the biggest mistake of her young life. Franco might have been a good lover, but he was far from an ideal husband.

'I just wanted him gone,' she said.

Within months of their marriage Franco and Anna Maria, who at one time only had eyes for each other, now embarked on extra-marital affairs. It was as if they needed to assert their independence of one another and further crush whatever bit of love was left in their relationship.

While Franco was working late in the chip shop, Anna Maria and her friend were dancing at Club 2000, a nightclub in the Spawell complex in Tallaght. There, just months after her marriage, she met a handsome barman called Peter Gifford.

At first they were just friends. He started calling to the chip shop in Rathfarnham, making sure beforehand that Franco wasn't there.

It became a regular Tuesday night outing: Anna Maria and three of the staff would go clubbing and Peter Gifford and some friends would join them.

They often talked about her husband. She told him about the violent marriage and alleged that Franco had beaten her with a baseball bat. He strung her along with stories that he could get someone to 'get rid' of her husband Franco and boasted of his connections. To Gifford it was only a joke – he was acting out a fantasy for her benefit. But to Anna Maria his promises were real. She fell for them, and for him.

Then one night she kissed him. It was as if she was wiping all traces of Franco from her life.

Gifford was hardly the passionate lover. 'I didn't go chasing her,' he said, as if such machismo was unbecoming of an Irish male. 'I don't cheat on a man,' he added mysteriously, having seduced the young newly wed.

But he was certainly cheating on the earthy, sexually driven Franco Sacco in those months of the summer of 1996.

As they lay together in bed Anna Maria told him how unhappy she was, trapped in a marriage with a man who beat her, who humiliated her in front of her friends and who was a bully and a liar.

Gifford was a man of the world and Anna Maria was a girl who wanted to get out of a troubled and violent marriage. She would cry into his shoulder and recount the latest episode in her marriage and the urgent need to find someone who would kill Franco. When she repeatedly asked if he had found anybody to 'do the job' he told her phoney stories of 'men on the run' and other improbable tales that anybody but a desperate young housewife would have seen through.

'How much will it cost?' she asked.

'About a thousand pounds,' he replied.

It was a figure Anna Maria understood. One night when she was out with a group she was introduced to a friend's brother, an up-and-coming gangster. He told her about the seamier side of Dublin life. The young man put on his best Mafia manners and made out that he knew what was going on in the underworld.

'Could you have someone killed?' she asked. Yes, he had replied, it could be done.

'How much?' she asked.

'A thousand,' he said.

She got the money together. He took it – and disappeared.

But now she felt her prospects were better. Peter Gifford told her he had connections – hinting that he knew people in the IRA who would organise 'the job'. It was a show of bravado, but the blonde young Irish-Italian certainly believed it could be organised.

Her affair with Gifford didn't last very long, but they stayed friends and she still hoped that he could organise someone to kill Franco. At Christmas 1996 she called to his house with a present, leaving a pair of gloves behind.

In January of 1997 the Rathfarnham shop mysteriously went on fire. Investigators believed that someone had tampered with the gas pipe in an attempt to kill Franco, who personally always lit the ovens at the beginning of the working day. It was never discovered who was behind the attempt on his life.

While Franco stayed behind in Dublin overseeing the rebuilding of the shop, Anna Maria and her young friend went off on a holiday to the sun. She was coming to rely more and more on her young friend who had by now moved into the Coolamber Park house with her and her husband.

Then Anna Maria herself got a shock when she discovered that her husband was having an affair with an Italian girl who had come from his own village to work in another chip shop in Dublin.

Late one night when he came home from work they started to talk. She told him she knew of his affair. Then she told him of her own affair with Peter Gifford. For once Franco did not lose his temper. Maybe he was just happy to get off so lightly himself. The two of them decided to give their marriage another chance and try to fall in love all over again.

But Franco just didn't have the temperament for a calm life. His moods swung violently from happiness to fury and Anna Maria didn't humour him.

One night in early March 1997, Franco was looking for sex, but Anna Maria refused as she had thrush. He took a belt and lashed out violently at her, hitting her on the arm.

'Lie down and take it or I'll kill you,' he yelled at her in Italian. As he raped her he was furious and struck her several times, but his pent-up emotions dissipated after the sex. He lay back, spent, and pulled all the clothes over to his own side of the bed leaving her naked and cold. She got up and went into the bathroom and smoked a cigarette.

As she sat on the toilet seat they argued. Anna Maria

complained about the beatings, threatening to get a barring order against him.

'Don't put a foot outside the door! And by the way, if you go to the police I'll kill you for sure. I don't care about the law in this country, the most I'd get for killing you would be seven years.'

'You'd get life,' she answered.

'You know what your problem is? You're Irish, you have no Italian blood in you,' he sneered at her.

When she woke in the afternoon of the following day, Franco had left for work. The fifteen-year-old came into the bedroom. She had listened, powerless, to the howling of her friend being raped by her husband the night before. She sat on the bed and they talked about what had happened. Anna Maria described the beating and already her puffed-up eye was turning dark from one of the blows inflicted by her husband.

'I'd love to kill him because of what he's doing to you,' the girl said, after listening to the story.

'I know. If only you knew the half of it.'

Before she went down to her mother in the Ranelagh chip shop later in the day she let down her blonde hair, which she usually wore in a pony tail, to try to cover her black eye.

'What happened?' her mother asked.

Suddenly Anna Maria blacked out, falling on the tiled floor. An ambulance was called and she was brought to St Vincent's Hospital. Anna Maria told staff what had happened but she refused to make an official complaint.

A week later she was still angry and hurt.

On March 18, 1997, a Tuesday, Franco celebrated his twenty-ninth birthday by going with some of his male friends to Little Caesar's, an Italian restaurant off Grafton Street, for a meal. Anna Maria was working that night.

The following night was quiet in the shop. Franco put on his leather jacket and said he was going out. He went up the street in Rathfarnham to another chip shop run by his friend Gio Dinardi. The two men had come to Ireland from the same part of Italy at around the same time.

They talked about football. Franco followed Inter Milan and his friend, Juventus and the two of them had a bit of banter as they went up to Dinardi's house to watch highlights of a European Cup match played that night.

The two friends also played football together for the Italian community team, Lazio. Franco played full back, and together they often went to matches abroad to see Italy play, and organised games against other Italian teams.

Dinardi thought that Franco looked as if he'd had a bad day.

'He was a hard man,' he said. 'Sometimes he was in a good mood, sometimes he was in a bad mood.'

That night he was in a bad mood. But it would have been worse had Franco known what was going on back at his own chip shop.

Franco had left Anna Maria, her sister Caterina and the teenage girl to do the late shift. Not long after he was gone Peter Gifford arrived, bringing with him the pair of gloves that Anna Maria had left in his house the previous Christmas.

The four of them talked and joked together, mostly at Franco's expense. As they discussed Anna Maria's husband they agreed that he had to die. But how would they get rid of the body?

'We'll chop him up and stick him in the oven,' joked Caterina.

But Anna Maria wasn't joking when she asked Peter Gifford if he had got in contact with his friend who he promised would do the job.

'Nah,' he answered, 'he's still on the run.'

Then the fifteen-year-old girl joined the conversation.

'I'll do it,' she said, matter of factly.

'Would you?' asked Anna Maria.

'Yeah,' answered the girl.

At about 1.30 a.m. Franco ordered a taxi to take him home to Coolamber Park where he sat down to watch a video of *Heat*. At about the same time his wife and her fifteen-year-old friend closed up the shop. Peter Gifford drove them towards Coolamber Park, still talking about 'getting rid' of Franco. He left them off around the corner from the house. He didn't want to be seen by the big, strong Italian.

But now the joking was over. Franco Sacco was living on borrowed time.

It was shortly after 11 a.m. the next morning when the gun went off in Franco Sacco's bedroom. Nobody heard the noise of the gun going off. Nobody saw the two girls wobble out the front door moments later and climb into the car.

Anna Maria, her ears still ringing with the sound of gunfire, drove down to the chip shop in Rathfarnham to carry out her husband's last order: to open the shop on time. But they couldn't get the gas ovens to work, so they put a sign on the door saying the shop was closed because of a gas leak. Then they drove over to Tallaght to the home of Peter Gifford. Anna Maria got out of the car and rang the front door bell. When he answered she asked if he would help her to get rid of her husband's body. Desperate to get rid of her from the front door of his father's house he told Anna Maria he would see what he could do and he would call her later.

The girls then picked up Caterina from her home in Kimmage. As they drove back to Coolamber Park they told her what had happened.

Anna Maria wouldn't go upstairs when they got to the house. But the other two did. Armed with buckets of warm water and Flash they marched up the stairs to begin the clean-up, like a scene from the film *Pulp Fiction*.

Franco was lying on a mattress in the upstairs bedroom. They began to clean up the blood and tissue and bits of his skull that were splashed on the walls and the floor. At one stage the drama became dark and macabre when Caterina came down the stairs laughing and chased Anna Maria with a yellow duster. On it was 'something soft and gooey' which turned out to be a fragment of her husband's brain.

'Get away from me with that,' Anna Maria shouted hysterically.

Her elder sister, a child at heart, was always doing that to her, picking up spiders and snails and chasing her.

Anna Maria left the house, telling the others, 'Make sure everything is perfect before I get back.'

All the time the dead Franco was lying face down in a lake of blood on the mattress.

After the girls grew tired of the cleaning and scrubbing they left the house again. This time they went down to the chip shop in Ranelagh.

The fifteen-year-old thought that Anna Maria told her mother what had happened. Orna Sacco said to the girl: 'You are not to bring her into it' referring to Anna Maria.

When they returned to Coolamber Park Anna Maria ventured up the stairs for the first time since she'd tied her shoelaces on the stairs that morning as she heard the gun go off.

'I kept thinking, no he's asleep, everything's okay.'

The room was dark, but she could see the pool of blood.

'I couldn't get out of the room quick enough. I was weak.'

As the other two girls dropped bits of Franco's brains and loose pellets from the shotgun cartridge down the toilet they could hear Anna Maria downstairs, vomiting.

'It's going to be all right; I have a gut feeling,' her young friend reassured her.

At about 4.30 p.m. that day Peter Gifford rang Anna Maria Sacco. Immediately she asked him if he had got anybody to help get rid of the body. He said he was still trying.

They began wrapping Franco up, swaddling his body in

layer after layer of bed linen, like an Egyptian mummy. But with each new layer they were bickering. The blame game was already beginning. Who was going to take the blame for the death of Franco Sacco?

At 7.26 p.m. that Thursday night the fifteen-year-old girl walked into the public office in Rathfarnham Garda Station.

'I shot Franco,' she told the startled policeman behind the counter. He thought it was a prank, but when she became hysterical he called for back-up to check it out.

Sirens blaring, a Garda car was dispatched to Coolamber Park. Within minutes they found the body in the upstairs bedroom. The house was cordoned off as startled neighbours looked on.

At 8.50 p.m. Anna Maria Sacco arrived back at her house. She looked surprised when she was told her husband was dead. She became hysterical and banged her head against the door and starting kicking it.

'No, no, no,' she chanted.

She certainly knew how to act the part of the grieving widow, although by now she had known for about ten hours that her husband had been murdered and she had actively tried to recruit friends to cover it up and get rid of the body.

It was an unseasonably warm night when state pathologist John Harbison went into the Saccos' bedroom at about 11.30 p.m. on Thursday, March 20. There was a heavily bloodstained mattress and pillow on the floor. Lying beside it was a substantial bundle of bedclothes.

In all, Franco Sacco's body was wrapped in eight

bedsheets, five padded quilts and duvet covers, an electric blanket and two hand towels.

But when they unwrapped the first sheet, a light blue in colour, they could see the gaping wound in Franco Sacco's head.

As each layer was unravelled the blood stains grew thicker and, nestling in the last, a hand towel, they found the empty cartridge case of the bullet that had killed Franco Sacco.

It had entered his skull just above the right ear and blown most of the top of his head off, ploughing a furrow through his skull.

The bullet that put an end to Franco Sacco's life also put an end to the friendship between his wife and her young friend. After she was charged with murder the fifteen-year-old girl claimed that on the morning that Franco Sacco was shot, his wife, Anna Maria, had come into her bedroom with the hunting rifle still in its case. Anna Maria had taken it out of the case and handed it to her.

'I couldn't do it,' she said of the moment she had stood outside Franco's bedroom.

'Please, just point it at him,' Anna Maria had pleaded with her.

The girl had gone into the room and pulled the trigger.

'His head, I got his head,' she cried coming out of the room.

But she said she hadn't even known it was loaded. 'I didn't know how to put the bullets in,' she said.

The girl was convicted of the murder of Franco Sacco and

sentenced to seven years in jail. Just a couple of months later, however, she was released because the State didn't have a suitable place of detention for her.

Anna Maria Sacco went through two trials, charged with the murder of her husband. The first ended with a hung jury. She was cleared in the second.

In all the high drama of the court cases there was one poignant moment. As Anna Maria outlined the violent nature of her late husband, suddenly a man stood up in the courtroom.

'You know that is not the truth and you're standing there telling lies!' he shouted. 'The girl shot Franco because of you.'

Anna Maria had another secret; she and Franco Sacco had something in common after all, although Franco was never to know. Some months after his death, his wife gave birth to a baby girl. Anna Maria didn't seem to see the irony when she named the baby Francesca – in his honour.

6

A LADIES MAN

She didn't want to go out with him ever again, but Sean just didn't know how to take no for an answer. He pestered her day and night. Then, when he turned up to do a tiling job in Frank's Bar, where she worked serving food, she knew it was hopeless. He was stalking her and he wouldn't give up until she surrendered and went on a date. So she agreed. But even as she said yes, she promised herself it would be the last time.

He picked her up that Saturday after she had finished early at the bar. The days were beginning to stretch in early April and it was still daylight that evening in 1997 as he drove out of the town of Tullamore, Co Offaly in his Ford Orion car. It was a bit clapped-out by now but he wouldn't part with it.

'She's a great yoke,' he used to say, rubbing his hands together, 'a great yoke altogether.'

He had picked their destination, a quiet lonely bogland wood called Shanderry, outside Portarlington, Co Laois. Almost immediately it began to bother her, she knew this road too well. Shanderry, 'the old bog' in Gaelic, was where they had first become lovers more than fifteen years before. How different it had been then. They would park his Mercedes and go for a walk over the soft turf. They would hold each other tight and kiss desperately in the whispering wood. Later in the back seat of the big car they would make passionate love.

Then he would go back to his wife and children and she would go back to her husband and children.

Back then their illicit moments together were filled with joyous sex and heart-stopping danger. They were both living on the edge; eventually they toppled over it.

Now as they drove along Sean wanted to wallow in the nostalgia of those long lost moments. All she wanted to do was to forget that she had lost everything – her children, her family, her friends – by falling for a loser.

His voice grew shrill as he pleaded, 'Why can't you move back in with me? I'll cut down on the drinking. It will be better this time.'

It was what she had been expecting. So she said 'no' with feeling and she kept repeating it.

But he continued to whinge. 'I need you, I can't live without you.'

'No,' she answered, 'I just can't go through it all over again.'

She didn't get annoyed about it any more. She was past that. Now she just wanted to be left alone to live her life in her own quiet way.

'I'll kill myself,' he threatened.

She wasn't going to fall for that one either. She didn't take it seriously. It was the kind of thing he said when he'd been drinking and was feeling maudlin. But she knew that Sean loved himself too much for that.

The argument was still unresolved when they reached Shanderry. He drove along the narrow path into the bog, surrounded by bullrushes and reeds and silver birch just coming into leaf.

They came to that lonely spot where they had once been lovers long ago. He stopped the car and turned off the ignition. He looked at her briefly but didn't say anything further. Getting out of the car, he moved around to the back while she sat there, her mind wandering back to those long lost days of lust and glory. She had sacrificed so much. For what? she wondered.

She opened the passenger door to breathe in the rich aroma of peat and decay. She couldn't see him but she heard the boot of the car opening. As he returned she turned in the seat to face him – and found she was looking down a gleaming gun barrel poking menacingly through the driver's window.

It was pointed directly at her face. She was stunned. It can't end like this, she thought.

'You must be joking,' she said with a smile. 'I will move back in with you.'

But his lips curled in contempt.

When they first met in 1982 Sean Brennan was a thirty-three-year-old successful married businessman with a string of kids like steps on a stairs. Bernadette Sherry was twenty-nine years old, a married mother of three, dissatisfied with the mundane life of a housewife and mother. She wanted excitement, and Sean Brennan gave it to her in spades.

He seemed to have it all. He had easy charm and money and she fell for his zest for life. He was one of those rare souls who seem to live every day as if it is their last.

He changed his Mercedes car every January, he had an apartment in Spain and, when it became more fashionable to own a villa, he bought one. He went to Cheltenham Races with a crowd of local businessmen where, their cases bulging with cash, they enjoyed the drinking, the gambling and the nightly high-stakes card games.

At home he didn't drive to Kilbeggan Races, he went by helicopter with a solicitor friend. He was welcomed into Mullingar Golf Club and, standing at the bar in his brightly coloured golf jumper, he impressed fellow club members with stories of how he was earning £4,000 a week.

Married with a young family he was already known as a man 'who fancied a bit of skirt' and he liked to boast about his conquests. 'I'm a bit of a ladies man all right,' he would confess.

Sean Brennan was living proof that if a man was smart and worked hard he could make it to the very top. He hadn't had it easy to start with. He trained as a carpenter and worked on the building sites at a time when there wasn't much money in the 'building game', as he called it. But when a couple of local businessmen started up a joinery firm he was the one with the expertise. The enterprise went well and he was appointed production manager and made a director of the firm. But Sean Brennan was getting a taste for the high life, and when he saw the amount of money that could be made he decided to strike out on his own.

He realised the fad for fitted kitchens and other quality furniture was here to stay and he started his own joinery company in Tyrellspass, Co Westmeath with his wife, Mary, as a fellow director. He took out a big loan with National Irish Bank and got down to business. Soon there was so much work he couldn't cope with it. He kept putting his prices up but the jobs kept rolling in.

Then something happened to Sean Brennan: he began to believe his own publicity. It was the '80s and 'greed was good'. It wasn't enough to have a thriving business and plenty of money. He wanted all the vulgar trappings that new money could buy, the big cars, the stylish apartment in Spain, the afternoons on the golf course, the long nights of drinking and the mornings enjoying the pleasures of a young mistress.

Although he marched up the aisle of his local church in Tyrrellspass with his family every Sunday, Sean Brennan now had a secret that only a few close friends would share.

In 1982 he met mother of three, Bernadette Sherry. Like many of his conquests it started as a casual affair. He was wealthy and carefree and he liked to show the girls a good time in the bars or at the races while his wife stayed at home and minded their children. But it turned out Bernadette wasn't like the other casual conquests. Oddly enough, it was love. Not that Sean Brennan was going to leave his wife or anything like that, but for a while he seemed to settle down, satisfied to have more children with his wife and still keep Bernadette as his lover.

However, Bernadette Sherry couldn't lead a double life like him. It became too much for her to bear so she left her husband and their three children and moved out of the house in Tyrrellspass.

Sean Brennan had no such qualms. During their affair he had a number of children with his wife, until finally he was the father of eight children.

But his lifestyle of drinking, gambling and carousing meant that he was no longer taking care of his business. He might have been acting the big fellah in the Golden Valley at Cheltenham, but back home his employees were leaving to set up their own companies – and taking the business with them. His customers were finding more reliable firms that paid more attention to the job.

'I was leading a double life the whole time. I was under terrible pressure,' said Sean Brennan. And the greater the pressure the more he buried himself in the drink.

He was also taking it out on his wife, Mary, and there was a history of drink-related domestic violence until 1994 when she finally got a barring order against him and he was thrown out of their house. By now his business was in ruins and Sean Brennan moved in with Bernie Sherry who was living in a flat in Tullamore.

It was a big comedown but every town in Ireland has its businessman who crashed to earth through a combination of alcohol and arrogance. Sean Brennan lived on past glories until the money ran out altogether. It got so bad that the once high-flying businessman could no longer even get a job as a carpenter. He was too well known as a drunk and a messer for anyone to trust him.

Even socially a lot of people couldn't stomach his boastful arrogance. Brennan was anxious to tell anyone who would listen of his conquests as a lover. He was also quick to take something up wrong and get involved in an argument and many people kept well away from him when he came into the pub. While people had put up with him when he had money, they began to shun him now that he had fallen from grace.

But Brennan was a good tradesman and he turned his hand to tiling to make a few bob. By this stage he had been 'done for drunken driving' so he relied on his lover, Bernie, to drive him from job to job. Their life together was on a downward spiral and Bernadette Sherry could stand it no longer.

Finally in early 1997 they had a row and she moved out of their flat. She found a place of her own outside the town of Tullamore and she put her name down with the council for social housing.

'If she gets a house she'll never move back with me,' Sean Brennan told a drinking companion crossly during a session.

He moved into a smaller flat on Church Road and began to stalk her. When she went out with friends he followed her. Sometimes when she was walking along the street in Tullamore he would suddenly appear, begging her to return.

Maybe he really loved her, or maybe she was the only one he had to cling to after the wreckage of his marriage and his business. But Bernadette had had enough.

If he had been flamboyant she was the opposite. In Frank's

Bar she did her job serving the food, but she never really got to know the customers like some people do. She kept to herself.

One day Sean Brennan came strolling into Frank's Bar asking for work. As it happened the owner, Frank Gillison, didn't know Sean Brennan and wasn't aware of his relationship with one of the waitresses. It also happened that he had some tiling work to be done and Brennan turned out to be a good tradesman.

'That's my woman downstairs,' he said to Frank one evening, which was the first indication the bar owner had that there was something between Sean and Bernadette.

What exactly the relationship was nobody knew, because Bernadette Sherry was keeping as far away from him as possible.

But now, working closely together in the pub, she could no longer avoid him and that's when she agreed to go to Shanderry with her one-time lover just to avoid his making a scene.

But unknown to his former lover Sean Brennan had made some preparations for the evening out. Earlier that week he had called to a cousin and paid him £30 for a gun and a couple of cartridges. He said he was going to get out a bit more and stay away from the pubs and that he intended to take up clay pidgeon shooting.

And that's how Bernadette Sherry ended up looking down the barrel of a gun at dusk in the remote bogland.

Trembling, she promised him that she would move back in

with him. But he could feel the fear and hesitation in her voice. Sean Brennan wasn't convinced.

And he was a coward. As he saw her cowering in the seat of the car he could feel the surge of power that such control gives a man with nothing left to lose. He didn't need to raise his voice, he didn't need to hit her. He held the power of life or death in his own hands.

He pulled the trigger.

The blast of the shotgun drove Bernadette out of the car and she fell in a heap on the bog road. Brennan walked around and left the gun leaning against the back bumper of the Ford Orion. He knelt down and cradled Bernie Sherry's head in his arms and cried.

'I love you,' he said and he kissed her.

She didn't say anything. Her body was heaving in pain and a dribble of blood trickled from the side of her mouth like a raindrop on a window pane.

Then he laid her down on the peat and picked up the rifle. He aimed and pulled the trigger again. This time the shot tore into her chest inflicting massive damage and killing her instantly. The lovers were now parted forever.

Sean Brennan bundled the body of Bernie Sherry into the boot of the car, her blood staining the back bumper as he heaved her limp corpse over the lip and into the trunk beside his spare tyre and his tiling tools.

Dusk had turned to darkness as he calmly got into the car and drove back to Tullamore. He parked in the car park behind Library Hall off Church Road, where he had his bachelor apartment. Using his shirtsleeve he rubbed the blood off the bumper, and then he went inside to his flat where he took all his clothes off and put them in a sack.

That night Sean Brennan did what he usually did on a Saturday night: he shaved and dressed carefully and then he went drinking. At different stages during the night he met three of his children. They were the older three, grown up now and leading their own lives. They bought him a drink and chatted.

He wanted to tell them what he'd done, but he couldn't. He just ordered another drink. Around him everyone was laughing and joking and telling stories and he joined in, no longer thinking of his lover curled up dead in the boot of his car just down the street.

The next morning he woke hung over and depressed. He took out the gun and looked at it. He thought about ending his own life.

'I just couldn't do it,' he said.

He rang his wife, Mary, on the telephone and told her what had happened. Then he rang the guards in Tullamore, the tears streaming down his face as he talked. While someone listened on the other end of the telephone, gardaí came around and broke into his flat, grabbing him before he could do anything further with the gun.

One of the detectives involved in the case shook his world-weary head and reckoned there was never much danger of suicide.

'Sean was too fond of Sean to kill himself,' he said, ruefully.

Instead he's doing life in prison for the murder of the woman he said he couldn't do without, the woman he shot in cold blood and whom he told 'I love you', as if that was some comfort as her life ran out on a lonely bog lane at Shanderry.

7

LITTLE GIRL LOST

The little blue-eyed girl was wearing her favourite Barbie knickers. The elastic was loose, the cotton cloth was worn thin and they were mildewed and discoloured with age. But for six-year-old Deirdre Crowley they were one of the few things that remained from a past that was fading fast from her memory. These little familiars reminded her of a time when she lived the normal life of a child playing with her cousins, feeding the ducks or simply walking along the street holding her mother's hand. It wasn't like that now.

She had been cooped up in this house for so long that she didn't even know what the outside world looked like any more. Her father called it home, but to her it was just like those prisons she read about in her fairy-tale books.

Sometimes when she pressed her pretty little face to the window of the damp gloomy house her father would rush into the room and pull her away from it. She lived now in her own little world, drawing stick figures with her colouring pencils as if she could no longer remember what real people even looked like.

In the long summer evenings she could hear children playing noisily in a garden somewhere in the distance. But

Deirdre daren't leave her lonely hidden world. There was just her and Dad, living in their little cocoon. He said it was a special place and she wanted to believe him but even at her young age she knew something must be dreadfully wrong.

Even in summer the house seemed damp, its windows nailed shut, the doors back and front bolted, the stale air swirling with little particles of dust when a ray of sunshine stole into her world.

Occasionally Bunny would call with some treats. She liked Bunny because here was a new face in her isolated little world. But even the treats didn't mean that much any more. Little Deirdre would have swapped all the chocolates and the toys just to be able to walk down a street into a park and to whoop with joy on the swing, like any other ordinary little girl.

But Deirdre had no such happy days. Hour after hour, day after day, week after week, month after month until it all seemed to merge into one long silent scream for a little girl clinging desperately to a few fading memories of a lost childhood.

Chris Crowley was brought up in Togher, a nice middle-class suburb of Cork city. A maths and languages teacher he had the precise and organised mind of a chess player. He got married briefly and lived in Glanmire, but the marriage didn't last. Chris Crowley was really only successful when he was preying on the young and impressionable. When his wife quickly tired of his obsessive controlling nature she simply disappeared from his life. He kept the house, renting it out and moving on to Fermoy, a bustling market town north of Cork city.

He was like a spider, always planning and plotting moves so far ahead that it seemed he could no longer enjoy the present. He looked at the world through narrow eyes thinking, what's in this for me?

Yet women found him attractive, particularly the younger ones. He preyed on the serious, intelligent girls, who melted before his silent intensity. In their innocence they mistook his obsessiveness for misunderstood genius. He exploited them mercilessly for sex and other favours and appeared to take a twisted pleasure in controlling their lives.

Regina Nelligan was one of his pupils at the Loreto convent in Fermoy, Co Cork. She was a shy, artistic, good-looking girl with dark eyes and long, dark hair. He seduced the sixteen-year-old girl during a school trip to Paris. She was infatuated with the romance of the city and fell for his fluency in the French language and his easy command of situations which others might find difficult. In her admiring eyes he could do no wrong. He was repaid when she came to his room at night for passionate sexual encounters.

She wasn't the only one.

He had a string of 'affairs' although in truth they were mostly casual relationships with young and impressionable women. He would instil in his conquests the value of loyalty and even after they parted he would keep in touch, always anxious about how they were doing and how they were coping without him controlling their world.

Some of them were grateful to get out of from under his pervasive influence. They cut the cord, not realising just how lucky they were.

But, like a moth drawn to the light, Regina Nelligan couldn't keep out of his orbit. There was something of a cult leader about the man. He inspired a blind kind of loyalty with his conviction and the certainty of his cause – whatever it happened to be. His mind was focused on what he wanted to achieve and if others got hurt that was no concern of his. Chris Crowley didn't have acquaintances; you were either in his tightly bound circle or you didn't really exist in his world.

Regina Nelligan's love affair with her teacher continued until she did her Leaving Certificate. He controlled her 'emotionally and sexually' to such an extent that he cut her off from her schoolfriends and other outside interests. Even her family found that the girl had become a distant stranger.

There was no room in their little world for anybody but each other. He was ten years older than her, but to the schoolgirl who had lived all her life in Fermoy he was a man of the world, sophisticated and knowledgeable.

Someday he was going to achieve something, he would tell her, but for the moment he was content to play the Master to his teenage charges.

To celebrate her Leaving Cert and the end of the school year they took off together on a holiday to Italy. Cooped up with Chris Crowley day and night, however, left Regina with a terrible feeling of claustrophobia. Out in the real world beyond the classroom she suddenly saw a different side to the man who had ruthlessly trained and nurtured her as a submissive lover. He didn't want her to meet or talk to other people as normal couples do on holidays. He wanted to possess her completely in body and soul until she could no longer endure the jealous rages and the awful confining world he inhabited. Their relationship ended, badly, somewhere in Italy.

Soon after they returned home she left Fermoy and went off to study in the National College of Art and Design in Dublin.

But Crowley never let anybody completely out of his web. In her first year in Dublin he contacted Regina and although they had ceased to be lovers they met several times.

Back in Fermoy to visit her parents, Regina Nelligan bumped into him on the street. They went for a quiet chat and they agreed they wouldn't see each other again. But then he made her enter into a pact: if either of them were ever in trouble they would be able to call on the other, and each would give unquestioning loyalty.

Of course, Crowley knew that it was a one way street – some day he might need her. He was already making plans even when he didn't know the objective.

It would be almost a decade before Chris Crowley contacted Regina Nelligan again, but such was his hold on her, so badly had he damaged the fragile schoolgirl psyche, that when he did call all those years later Regina Nelligan came running.

After their affair had ended he 'jumped from one

relationship to another, as a betrayal of Regina' according to one of her schoolfriends. Then in the spring of 1994 Chris Crowley went on a holiday to India, and there met Christine O'Sullivan from Ballydesmond in north Cork.

A good-looking woman she came from a tightly knit family of sisters and there was something more mature and appealing about her than his schoolgirl conquests. In Christine he found someone who, like him, was searching for something in life. Brought up in a devout Catholic family she had lost her way with the church, but she was searching for something to bring a spiritual dimension back to her existence.

At first she found it in Chris Crowley. His obvious intelligence and intensity impressed her. They became lovers and on August 11, 1995, Christine gave birth to their beautiful baby, Deirdre.

It was the most wonderful moment of Christine's life – and Chris Crowley shared it with her. The serial womaniser became the doting dad. Little Deirdre filled some deep-seated need he had for permanence in his life and quite soon she became more important to him than the relationship he had with her mother.

Gradually, over a four-year period, Christine O'Sullivan began to get a glimpse into the dark and hateful world of Chris Crowley. The break-up of their relationship was nasty and bitter – and little Deirdre was at the centre of the family feud.

Christine O'Sullivan moved on and found what she was

looking for in a small Baptist community near her home in the Cork suburb of Douglas. She was impressed by the fact that it involved more than just going to Mass on a Sunday and forgetting about religion for the rest of the week. These were people who really prayed together, shunned the material pleasures of drink and drugs, yet still remained regular members of the community in which they lived.

But that wasn't the way Chris Crowley saw it. He told friends that their relationship had broken up because Christine had joined 'a cult' and that his daughter was being brainwashed and indoctrinated. In fact what really disturbed him was that Christine was involved with something he couldn't control.

Solicitors were brought in to sort out his visitation rights and the details of his access to his daughter. Then in early 1999 he began to plot. Nothing was ever a spur of the moment decision with him. Like a chess master looking at the pieces on a chequered board he began to work out each move with meticulous care and attention to detail.

But he knew he couldn't do it all himself. Looking back at those who had pledged their souls to him, he saw Regina Nelligan's willing features and knew he would use her.

First he sold his house in Cork and cashed in a couple of insurance policies he had been paying into over the years. He put the proceeds into a secret bank account which would give him – and a couple of trusted friends – access to over a hundred thousand pounds in cash. Then, when he took his daughter Deirdre, now three, on visits, he began to accumulate little items of her possessions, toys, a coat or a spare pair of knickers, shoes or a teddy bear.

Looking back on it Christine O'Sullivan realised that when Deirdre came home from her days with her dad something was frequently missing. But she put it down to male fecklessness rather than the calculating mind of a disturbed and jealous father. By the time she realised what was really going on it was too late.

With most of the chess pieces now in place Crowley sent a letter to Regina Nelligan at her Dublin address. He asked her to meet him and he suggested the rendezvous take place at the shopping centre just outside Portlaoise, about halfway between Dublin and Cork. They hadn't seen each other for over eight years but Crowley, like a Russian spymaster, was reawakening the sleeper he had planted so many years earlier.

It was a July day when they sat in the anonymous coffee shop and renewed their friendship. Whatever love there had been was gone, he was now using her for his own ends, playing on the emotional fragility he had helped to inculcate in her all those years before.

'I need help,' he pleaded. He told Regina that the mother of his little girl was suffering from post-natal depression and wasn't able to look after Deirdre. He told her that Christine was ill and involved in a cult, and he needed to get Deirdre away from her, 'for my daughter's sake.'

'Regina, you're the only one who can do this for me,' he pleaded. 'Deirdre is being brainwashed in this cult and there's no telling where it will all end. They could go off to South

America or some obscure place like that and I'll never see her again.'

It was a convincing story and as she listened Regina Nelligan was drawn back again into Chris Crowley's tangled web.

He told her his plan and what she needed to do. Money, he said, was no object. He would do anything to save his daughter from this fate. He had other friends who would be discreet, but they lived too close to home in Fermoy. He needed someone on the outside who would escape suspicion.

Regina Nelligan went back to Dublin and began to carry out his orders. She made phone calls to auctioneering firms around the country until her search was narrowed down to Clonmel, Co Tipperary. After sifting through several properties on offer she agreed to rent Croan Lodge, a small but detached house surrounded by high walls and without windows facing the road. It was a bit gloomy and isolated for most people's taste, but Regina Nelligan knew it was the ideal hideout for Chris Crowley.

Using a false name she agreed to rent the property on a long-term basis and have the money paid directly to the landlord through a standing order in the bank so that there was no direct contact between them.

Summer turned to autumn and the planning continued. All the while Chris Crowley kept up an appearance of normality. Although the break-up with Christine had been acrimonious Crowley now began to worm his way back into the affections of the mother of his child. Suddenly he was pleasant and friendly. Sometimes they even did things together with Deirdre, normal things parents do, like bringing their child swimming or going for walks in the woods on a Sunday afternoon.

But Chris Crowley didn't want to share his child with anyone, especially her mother.

In the first week of December solicitors for both Chris Crowley and Christine O'Sullivan finally reached an agreement on visitation rights. The little girl was allowed to stay overnight with her father once a week.

Crowley drove to Douglas on that Friday evening of December 3, 1999, and picked Deirdre up for their first weekend together as father and daughter. He promised Christine that Deirdre would be back the following evening.

He also had promises for Deirdre: staying up late watching television, visiting friends who had children her own age and other treats that would make it a night to remember.

Deirdre kissed her mother goodbye.

'See you tomorrow,' Christine O'Sullivan said to her daughter as she knelt down and tugged her coat closed and kissed her. Shutting the door of the car she saw the little face of her four-year-old pressed against the window and her hand waving.

'Bye Mammy, bye, love you.'

Down the road Chris Crowley pulled over and took out a pay-as-you-go mobile phone he had bought earlier that week. He was careful that way: he'd never talk on the phone while driving the car. He phoned Regina Nelligan in Dublin. The conversation was short and brief.

'It's on,' he said. 'Meet me in the car park of the Talbot Hotel in Wexford.'

Then, instead of setting out for Fermoy where little Deirdre had been expecting to spend the night, he headed east across country through the towns of Youghal and Dungarvan and New Ross and on towards Wexford. He stopped only briefly to buy some groceries and a pair of shiny new shoes for the little girl.

When he reached the Talbot Hotel Regina Nelligan was already there, sitting in her parked car in a distant part of the car park. Crowley drove in and waited until there was nobody around, then quickly and without fuss he put the little girl into the back of Regina Nelligan's car. He transferred her few belongings and his holdall into the boot and the three of them drove off towards Clonmel and a new life of hiding out in Croan Lodge.

Anyone else would have seen the pointlessness of this existence. Crowley had the child now, but he had no life and neither did she, holed up in isolation, unable to venture outside to feel the rain or smell the flowers or to play with other little kids. But in Chris Crowley's twisted mind this was enough. He had someone to control, even if it was only a four-year-old girl who suddenly didn't know what was going on in her life.

Three days after Crowley had taken Deirdre, Regina Nelligan posted a letter for him to the principal of the Loreto College in Fermoy requesting an immediate career break.

She also made a series of phone calls leaving 'coded messages' to a colleague in the school, the school caretaker and a relative. Crowley was letting them know that he had his daughter and he would be calling on them when he needed their help.

Christine O'Sullivan was frantic. Initially when her little girl didn't come home she didn't really worry, but as the hours and the days passed her mind began to go back over things and it didn't take long to work out that she had been the victim of an elaborate and cruel deception.

On Christmas Eve Chris Crowley's car was found in the Talbot Hotel. A few days later the police in Cork got an anonymous phone call telling them that a man and a young girl had been seen taking the ferry from Rosslare to Fishguard, in Wales.

Crowley and little Deirdre settled down to a life of tedium and hiding, 'a life of deceit and loneliness,' as described by one of his friends.

The little girl had a television set and a few videos. But her father didn't want to go out and rent any new ones, because it would only arouse suspicion. Every so often 'Bunny', as Deirdre was told to call Regina Nelligan, would arrive with a gift of new toys and videos. She also came laden down with groceries from the carefully compiled lists that calculating Crowley had drawn up. Everything, he insisted, must be paid for with cash so there would be no trail.

It was a terribly lonely and depressing life for anybody, let alone a lively little four-year-old who wanted to play with her

Barbie dolls and with other little girls her own age. The physical hardship she had to endure was nothing compared to the mental torture of living isolated and shut up in the damp house surrounded by trees.

But there was an even more sinister side to the story, of which even Crowley's accomplice, Bunny, was completely unaware. In the long holdall he had brought to Croan Lodge was a shotgun he had acquired from the school caretaker in the Loreto convent. A double-barrelled shotgun.

Sometime during the long nights in hiding he had carefully sawn off the barrels of the gun as well as the butt of the stock so that he was left with a compact, lethal weapon that was easy to hide and easy to use. He had wrapped two layers of electrical tape around the butt to give him a good grip. The sporting gun was now a weapon made for destruction at close quarters.

Always calculating the odds, Chris Crowley had also brought three black-handled long-bladed knives and placed them at strategic points: one was in the shed, another on the mantelpiece of the living room out of harm's way from his daughter, and the third on top of a wardrobe in his bedroom. Chris Crowley did not intend to let anyone take his daughter from him.

Christine, however, never gave up hope and continued to campaign to find her daughter. A year after her disappearance she made a heartfelt plea to Pat Kenny on the *Late Late Show* on RTE for anyone with any knowledge of her daughter to come forward to the police. She knew in her heart that

Crowley was getting help.

Besides Regina Nelligan, a small group of Crowley's close friends were helping to keep Deirdre in her father's dungeon. Without them he would not have been able do it.

But after nearly twenty months there was still no sign of him or the little girl. It was as if they had just disappeared off the face of the earth. There was talk that he might have gone to France, because of his fluency in the language. Others maintained eastern Europe was more likely as it was just then opening up to a new wave of Irish businessmen buying property behind what had once been the Iron Curtain.

As people talked endlessly, speculating on where he might have gone, the name Regina Nelligan was mentioned. Christine was intrigued by the connection between the sixteen-year-old lover and the father of her child.

'I had never met her and I'd never even heard of her until some months after Deirdre disappeared and this name popped up,' she said. 'I hadn't heard about any of his affairs,' she added.

Detectives slowly but surely were building up a picture of this obsessive man. They too got to hear of his affair with Regina Nelligan. Two detectives from the National Bureau of Criminal Investigation called around to her flat in Dublin on the evening of August 4, 2001. They explained that they were investigating the disappearance of Deirdre and did she know anything that might be helpful.

'What kind of person do you think I am? If I knew where the child was I would tell you,' she answered, outraged.

Greg Fox pictured with his wife, Debbie, and their two boys
in their shop. When Debbie told him she was leaving him,
Greg Fox killed them all and tried to commit suicide.
(Independent Newspapers)

Maeve Byrne was stabbed to death in her
own home by her husband, Stephen.
(Independent Newspapers)

After stabbing his wife, Maeve, Stephen Byrne
drove his car off the pier in Duncannon, Co Wexford,
and drowned himself and their two children.
(Independent Newspapers)

Pat Gillane is led away after he was convicted of
conspiracy to murder his wife, Philomena.
(Independent Newspapers)

Bridie Gordon and her brother Martin.
Their sister Philomena was murdered
and stuffed into the boot of her own car.
(Independent Newspapers)

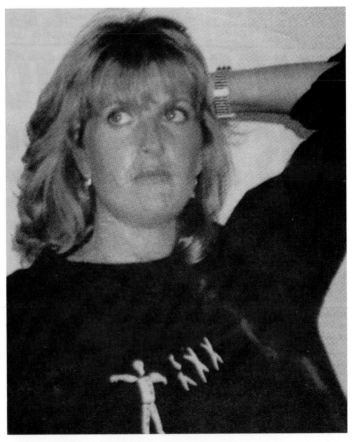
Patricia O'Toole: a Friday night out ended in violent death.
(Independent Newspapers)

Brian O'Toole at the funeral of his wife, Patricia.
(Independent Newspapers)

Anna Maria and Franco Sacco on their wedding day,
May 25, 1995. It was Anna Maria's nineteenth birthday.
(Independent Newspapers)

Anna Maria Sacco, cleared of murdering
her husband after two trials in Dublin.
(Independent Newspapers)

Lorraine Farrell lured her drug-dealer lover,
Paddy Farrell, to his death.
(Independent Newspapers)

Christine O'Sullivan with a few of the remaining
possessions of her murdered daughter, Deirdre Crowley.
(Independent Newspapers)

David Murphy thought he was too smart to be caught for the murder of his wife, Patricia.
(Independent Newspapers)

Happier days: Patricia Murphy, her mother Biddy Behan, her husband David, and their three children, pictured shortly after they moved to Dublin.

(*Independent Newspapers*)

Alison Shaughnessy, stabbed 54 times in her London flat.
(Independent Newspapers)

Joyce Quinn: a simple act of kindness led to her murder.
(Collins Photo Agency)

At his trial Kenneth O'Reilly muttered one word, 'sorry'.
(Collins Photo Agency)

She was a good actor and it was perhaps a convincing performance. But one of the detectives, glancing around the sparsely furnished flat, spotted newspaper cuttings of Chris Crowley's abduction of his daughter. They knew they were onto something, but didn't quite know what.

They began the slow process of getting Regina Nelligan's mobile phone records. They also noted a phone box near her flat and they contacted Eircom, who came up with an exhaustive list of telephone numbers.

When detectives came across the phone numbers of auctioneers in Clonmel on her mobile phone records and found the same numbers had been rung from the pay phone, they realised it was too much of a coincidence.

A few calls to Clonmel and the name of Croan Lodge suddenly came up in the conversation.

The scent was hot. Regina Nelligan was the prime suspect.

August 30, 2001, was a warm, pleasant summer's day. People were going off to the seaside, enjoying the long weekend, joining friends for a barbeque. But Chris Crowley, dressed in his usual tracksuit and loafers, padded around the semi-darkness of Croan Lodge. Deirdre wasn't feeling very well. Confined to the enclosed house for so long without fresh air had left her weak and sickly. He'd opened a cough bottle and given her two spoons and she slept most of the morning.

It was just another day to get through. Sometimes when Regina came he was able to go into Clonmel to get a few things, mostly for himself. He didn't buy anything for Deirdre as that might draw attention to them. But it was enough to get out for a few hours, just to hear the buzz of traffic and the sound of people talking and laughing on the streets of the town. It was a simple pleasure that he continued to deny his daughter.

Deirdre got up late and the two of them had a sandwich together. Although she was only six she was a bright child and he had converted one of the rooms upstairs to a study where they worked out maths puzzles.

That same morning Christine Crowley thought of her little girl as she went about her business. She thought of her every morning, and this morning seemed no different. Then in the early afternoon she got the most wished for phone call.

'We think we've found Deirdre,' the familiar voice of the detective told her.

The police investigating the case admired the young mother who had borne the loss of her daughter with a calmness and lack of hysteria that they didn't often encounter. Among themselves they had made an agreement that they would one day find the little girl. They owed it to her mother.

Christine O'Sullivan's heart leapt with the news. Throughout the ordeal she had never lost hope, but she had often wondered in those long weeks and months that followed. Now, more than twenty months later, there was the first glimmer of hope since they had been put on a false trail shortly after Deirdre disappeared.

'Don't say anything for the moment, but things are moving. Just stay by the phone, we should have news in the next few hours,' she was told.

As she was getting this exciting news two detectives in plain clothes walked around Croan Lodge. They tried to peer in through the downstairs windows but they were grime-stained and gave no clue if there was anyone in. Eventually they walked up to the front door and knocked.

The door opened cautiously and a bearded man wearing a baseball cap opened it, first only a sliver, but wide when they identified themselves as policemen. Chris Crowley had gone over this encounter in his mind time after time.

'There's been a few burglaries around the place,' one of the detectives told him, playing for time. 'Everything okay for you?' they asked, trying to look into the gloom of the interior for any signs of life.

'Fine, yeah, nothing strange,' Crowley answered in a Cork lilt. He was a good bluffer and he wasn't giving anything away.

The detectives decided to walk away and consider their next move.

But Chris Crowley, the chess player, was already one move ahead of them. He knew what they were looking for. He also knew that they knew he was the man they wanted. After twenty months he may even have been relieved that this sad and depressing game of adult hide-and-seek was at last over. Now he knew what he had to do.

When he'd taken possession of Croan Lodge Chris Crowley had thought very carefully about how to fortify it. He wanted to protect himself and his daughter from prying eyes or any sudden attempt to free the kidnapped child. Regina

Nelligan had picked Croan Lodge because there were no windows facing on to the road, instead it faced out on to the countryside. Crowley had nailed the downstairs windows closed, and against the back door he'd built a mound of briquettes, which blocked the entrance but gave the appearance of normality.

As the detectives walked across the road to consider their next move Crowley bounded back into the house and grabbed Deirdre. He dragged and pulled her so violently into the little yellow-painted utility room inside the front door that he left the imprint of his four fingers on her legs.

Holding the shotgun in his hand he climbed onto the toilet seat and peered out the small window to see what was going on out on the road.

'What do we do?' the detectives were asking each other as they crossed the road. They knew that somewhere in the dark, damp house was the six-year-old girl they were searching for. They turned to walk back towards the house.

Suddenly they heard the muffled roar of a shotgun. They jumped the wall and smashed their way through the back door facing the road and scrambled over the scattered briquettes. As they did so a second shot exploded in the little laundry room.

The detectives pushed open the door to find the two bodies slumped over the shotgun. The floor, the walls and the door of the airless room were spattered with freshly spilled blood. A cloud of blue smoke hung in the stale air over the death scene.

In his last moments Chris Crowley had jumped from the toilet seat and crouched down. With the barrel of the gun pointed at his little daughter's face, he pulled the trigger of the snub-nosed weapon. The blast blew most of her face away so that when her mother saw her corpse later she could only be identified by her eyes.

Having killed his daughter, Crowley reloaded. He held the sawn-off shotgun to his own skull and used the thumb of his left hand to pull the trigger. The bullet went through his cheek into the left side of his head, blowing out his left eye. He did not die instantly. He was still clutching the shotgun when the detective touched his body to make sure he was dead.

The state pathologist, Dr John Harbison, giving evidence at the inquest into Deirdre's death reported,

> Deirdre Crowley was facially unidentifiable because of the damage to her head. She wore a vest, blue knee-length trousers and Barbie knickers. She also had sandals on.
>
> She was a normal, well-developed female child. Her face was turned to the left. The entry of the bullet wound was to the front of the neck, above the breastbone. There was slight burning of the skin at the shotgun wound. There was also a large gaping wound on the head where the bullet exited. Her face and right cheek had to be replaced. Her ear was blown off and her eyes were undamaged, bar some damage to one of the sockets.

The impact of the single shotgun blast shattered her skull in fifteen places. To this day Christine O'Sullivan believes that Crowley deliberately shot little Deirdre in the face as one last act of revenge, so that her mother could never see her as she really was and remember her that way.

Amid the carnage there was one call to be made. For the detective involved it was the hardest he'd ever had to make in his life.

Waiting at home Christine O'Sullivan was imagining what it would be like to see her little girl again. What would she look like now, after all those long months?

> I was thrilled. I was walking on air. But at the same time I was hoping that everything would be all right and already thinking ahead that this could be difficult for Deirdre, coming home and facing all the people she hadn't seen for so long. My mind was racing ahead, planning things for her.

But then the detectives called. Christine O'Sullivan's dreams, her hopes and expectations of just an hour ago were in ruins.

All she could plan now for her little daughter, Deirdre, was a funeral.

8

LIFE AND DEATH
OF A PEN FRIEND

After her little daughter Alana went to bed Gloria sat at the kitchen table, opened her copy of the magazine and began to compose. Her hand poised above the paper, she thought for a moment, What should I say? and then as she scanned the other lonely hearts advertisements for ideas it came to her in a rush of inspiration.

> Destination Donegal: Sincere young woman WLTM caring man interested in relationship. Enjoy music, SD, children and dogs. Photos and phone number please.

She looked again at the magazine and checked the abbreviations. WLTM meant 'would like to meet' and SD stood for 'social drinker'. She checked that she had spelled the words correctly, got out her few pounds and addressed the envelope.

She wondered about the reference to children. Would whoever read it get the message that she had a child, the beautiful little girl sleeping soundly in the room above? Would it bother him? She knew from bitter experience that it put some men off when they learned she had a little girl. Others seemed to take it a different way, assuming for some reason that she was easy and available. But Gloria wasn't like that and maybe that was one of the reasons she was putting this notice in the little magazine.

She looked up and down the Personals once more. Down in one corner of the page her eyes fell again on a highlighted message under the warning 'Take Care'.

> It pays to take care when making contact:
> Always arrange to meet in a public place.
> Don't be afraid to say no if the meeting has not
> turned out the way you had hoped.
> Tell a relative or close friend where you are
> going and what time you will return.

The words were very simple, innocent almost. But it was a message that she noted. There were people out there who read these kinds of advertisements so that they could prey on the lonely and the vulnerable.

Then she wondered what people – friends and family – would think if they knew. She had joked about it before but she had always been too embarrassed to do anything more. 'You aren't that desperate,' some of her friends said in amazement. But in a way she was that desperate. At twenty-five all she wanted was love and affection.

After she put the envelope on the shelf to post in the morning she thought about the kind of men who would read it. Would they be old farmers who had never left home and spent their years minding their parents until their own lives were almost over? Would they be losers of one kind or another? Or just sad men who hadn't enough confidence to go to a dance or chat up a woman in a bar?

Then she wondered would there be weirdoes out there. Of course there would. But they wouldn't be the kind to read a magazine like this. The biggest worry of all was, well, would anyone bother to reply? But they did. That's how Gloria McCole found Eddie Harkin, through the Pen Friends column of *Ireland's Own.*

It's a strange little publication that appears to offer neither great excitement nor indeed the prospect of love and passion. It doesn't make any promises or boasts. It simply takes these advertisements from lonely people on trust that they are genuine. And they usually are.

There is nothing glossy or modern about it. Its origins lie in a time before television when families sat around the kitchen table in the country. In the fading light they played a game of cards, like Twenty-Five, or took the weekly *Ireland's Own* down from the shelf to read out bits and pieces that had been missed the previous evening.

That's one of the reasons Gloria McCole picked it. It had always been in the house when she was growing up and now she bought it every week out of habit – and of course to scan the Pen Friends column on the inside back cover.

There had always been a Pen Friends column in *Ireland's Own,* putting people overseas in touch with Irish people who wanted to correspond. That was in a time when people wrote to each other, out of curiosity or loneliness. But in recent years it had taken on a new lease of life. It was a way for people who wanted love or attachment to find someone like themselves.

There was nothing very sexy about it. Many of those who advertised made it clear they were devout RC (Roman Catholic) but still, there was always an element of mystery about such advertisements.

If there was murder associated with the magazine then it was to be found in one of the fictional stories that dots its old-fashioned pages and not a real-life murder mystery among its readers. But fact, as they say, is often stranger than fiction.

The advertisement was an easy and anonymous way of finding someone. Putting the advertisement in rather than replying to one already in the magazine gave her control of the situation. If there were any replies then she could sift through them herself and pick and choose.

She didn't hold out any great hope. It might work and then again it might not, but people who meet through such advertisements don't have unrealistic expectations. They really want to make it work, and often it does.

What surprised Gloria McCole and thirty-four-year-old Edmund 'Eddie' Harkin when they first met was how normal they both appeared to be. He had read the advertisement thinking, this is too good to be true, and she had the same reaction when she got his letter of reply and his photograph.

What dark secret, each wondered, could the other be hiding?

After they met and talked and quizzed each other about

why they had chosen to meet this way there didn't seem to be anything obvious. Gloria didn't keep her little daughter a secret, she was too proud of her for that, and Eddie seemed a normal kind of guy.

He was a taxi driver in Derry and read all kinds of stuff while waiting at the taxi ranks. He read the newspapers and, occasionally, magazines you wouldn't want to be seen with. Other times he read things that were discarded in the back seat of the cab, books and so on.

That was how he had unexpectedly come across *Ireland's Own*. Leafing through the pages he realised that here was a way of finding women who didn't know his secrets or his past. They would be open to his charm and would not be looking to find fault with him like everybody else. They were usually women 'of a certain age' just looking for a little bit of love and tenderness.

He swore this time he wouldn't go off the rails. He was even more determined after he met Gloria McCole. She was stunning looking and when he saw her across the crowded hotel bar for the first time he couldn't believe his luck. Eddie Harkin could be a charming man when he wanted to be and Gloria McCole desperately wanted it to work. Whatever it was, there was chemistry between them that first night and they agreed to see each other again.

Life seemed to hold out such promise when Gloria McCole was growing up as a young girl in Dungloe, Co Donegal. She came from a family of seven and she was close to her sisters. She was a handsome girl with big eyes and an honest, open face. As a teenager she liked to do all the things that teenagers enjoyed, dressing up and going out to the pictures and dances and having a good time.

Then, when she was nineteen years old and just out of school, she got pregnant and had a baby daughter, Alana. It wasn't easy for a single mother then. She was still very young and although she had help and support she also had responsibilities. So it seemed to her that part of her life passed her by as she was rearing the young baby.

As they grew into their twenties her friends had boyfriends and got married, but Gloria stayed single looking after her daughter and hoping the right man would come along. She moved into a house in the nearby town of Letterkenny where she got a clerical job with Telecom Eireann.

Like many women her age Gloria was longing for love. She didn't find it in the clubs or the dancehalls of bustling Letterkenny, a student town where you are considered old once you passed the age of twenty-one. The men were all too young for her or they were already married. Gloria was looking for the real thing. That's when she put the advertisement in *Ireland's Own*.

Eddie Harkin was pleasant without being either good looking or dapper. He was a homely type and he seemed to get on with most people. When he was with Gloria, in those early days, he was kind and gentle.

He treated Gloria like a lady and when he met her daughter he behaved properly. He genuinely loved children. He neither made an issue of the fact that Gloria had the little girl nor did he treat her as if she was somehow different. His biggest problem was hiding his own secret.

Eddie Harkin had a serious drink problem. He'd been a heavy drinker since the age of sixteen. Growing up in the troubled city of Derry hadn't been easy for him and he suffered from a cycle of alcoholism and depression.

Caught in the midst of the Troubles and the deeply sectarian nature of the place where he lived, he had avoided trouble on the streets but had found it in the bottle instead. Derry was a depressing city at the time, with its bombed-out buildings, violence likely to flair at any moment, and friends who either left the place altogether or got themselves involved in the Troubles. It was also a town blitzed by the economic blight of the Thatcher years, which saw much of its traditional industries closed down.

Eddie Harkin had lost part of his life – to the booze. Looking back he thought of all the times he had sat on a barstool drinking himself into oblivion, and he wished for something better. He was still drinking heavily when he picked up *Ireland's Own* and skimmed through it sitting in his cab one day. Fate must have played some part in their first meeting.

Eddie was a good actor. When he was with Gloria those first months he minded his drinking and kept his problem well hidden from the woman who had fallen so in love with him. But he wasn't being honest. He gave no indication of his drink problem never mind how serious it was or how easily it spiralled out of control into bitterness and violence.

Within a few months they decided that they had wasted enough of their lives already and they got married the following February at a small wedding attended by family and close friends.

The first few months were wedded bliss. Eddie Harkin loved his wife's daughter Alana, then five years old, and was anxious to have children of his own. The couple, now living in Letterkenny, very soon had a baby son of their own whom they named Joseph. Life had certainly taken a turn for the better as far as the newly married Gloria Harkin was concerned.

But her husband couldn't keep up the front. After the birth of their son, Eddie began to fall back into his old ways drinking heavily, coming home drunk and taking his temper out on his new wife.

The old saying 'if you want to know me, live with me' took on a frightening reality for Gloria. It wasn't long before she realised she was married to a man she didn't really know at all.

She confided in her sisters, telling them different parts of her harrowing story, how Eddie was drinking too much, that she had discovered to her horror that he was a violent man who regularly beat her. She was giving each of them parts of the jigsaw of her life. But none of them was seeing the full picture of how her little advertisement in *Ireland's Own* had frighteningly led to her life being dominated by a man who suffered from alcoholism and depression.

Gloria never came out and said exactly what was going on. She was too proud. A couple of times in their third year of marriage she could suffer the abuse no longer and took the children and went to stay with one of her family. But each time she returned. Each time he promised that he would give up the drink for good and they would have another go. And each time she believed him and prayed that it would turn out all right and they would have a normal family life.

Because of his drinking and argumentative nature the taxi company that employed Eddie Harkin had sacked him. He was now drawing the dole, living off money he sponged from his wife and spending most of his time in the bars of Letterkenny. It was a sad downward spiral. When he came home the rows would start and he would lash out, beating his wife and frightening their children.

The Christmas of 1990 was fearful and after four years of marriage Gloria could stand it no longer. She vowed that in the New Year she was going to get rid of him for good and start a new life on her own with the two children.

After a particularly bad episode she got a protection order against him and he went back to live in Derry. Despite their troubles Gloria still had some sort of grudging love for him and not even she could deny he really did love the children. He missed them desperately. He was, after all, the father of one of them.

That February, although they were no longer living together, they sent each other Valentine's Day cards. It was a naive and innocent, thing to do. But for Gloria that little natural act of love was to have fatal consequences.

A few weeks later when he called to the house one day to

meet the children they had a row and he raised his hand and lashed out, hitting her across the face.

'That's it,' she said, 'you're gone and you'll only see the children when I say so.'

She went to the Family Court for a barring order. When the judge was told about the Valentine's Day cards he decided not to grant it. He'd seen it all before; in a couple of weeks they would be in to have the barring order lifted and the whole cycle would start all over again. Instead, Eddie Harkin was allowed to take his son, Joseph, to Derry once every four weeks with the agreement of his estranged wife. Sometimes Alana went with them, she liked the excitement of the city.

On a May morning Gloria Harkin was ironing clothes for Alana, now nine, and Joseph, aged three. They were going off with Eddie that lunchtime for their monthly stay in Derry. Gloria was looking forward to a quiet weekend of her own, meeting friends without the pressure of her young son clinging to her. A night off would help ease the stress in her life.

Eddie had been off the drink for three months and, while she knew he was doing very well, she also knew that when he called he'd be asking her if he could come back to live in the house. She wasn't looking forward to that bit.

'Let's just try it again,' he had said to her in a phone call one evening. She had refused. Life had handed down just one disappointment too many and Eddie Harkin was it. She couldn't go through it all again, the drinking and the beatings and the awful uncertainty about his depression and his temper.

There was a knock on the door. It was Eddie. She wasn't expecting him so early. The children were dressed but she was still ironing Joseph's pyjamas and spare clothes and hadn't got his bags packed yet. She always wanted him to look his best whether he was at home or with his father in Derry.

She met Eddie at the door and the children came running out to greet him too. They were excited to be off because he really had a way with them, and they knew he would spoil them rotten.

Eddie still had no job and the money was tight so Gloria gave him a ten pound note and asked if he would take the children down the town for lunch while she got Joseph's things ready for the trip.

'No bother,' he said, with a smile.

As usual Alana, Joseph and Eddie had a great time and when the meal was over Eddie Harkin drove back up to the house which was in an estate outside Letterkenny.

'Alana, you look after the wee lad for a minute while I go inside and talk to your mother,' he said.

Gloria had the bags packed and waiting in the hall. She was about to go out to the car to give the children a kiss goodbye when Eddie appeared in front of her.

'Gloria, why can't we try to start all over again?' he pleaded.

'No!' she shouted.

'Gloria, I love you.'

She turned and walked back towards the kitchen. He followed her, still talking. He told her he was finished with the drink and hoped to get a job. Could they not give it another go?

'No,' she answered again.

'Well then I'm going to look for custody of wee Joseph – he's my son too. I can't bear this, just seeing him once a month. It's not right and its not natural. You're not getting the kids,' he said, with finality.

Eddie Harkin grabbed his wife. He tried to kiss her but she pushed him away. As she did so he grabbed a kitchen knife from the counter behind her and plunged it into her chest so violently that the blade broke in her body. He then grabbed another knife and stabbed her repeatedly, in the head, in the chest, in her lower body. He stabbed her fourteen times.

Alana heard the screams of her mother and ran into the house where she found Gloria lying dying on the floor of the kitchen.

'Help me,' she begged her distraught nine-year-old daughter.

But nobody could help her now. Gloria Harkin died there on the floor. Time had finally run out for a sad and lonely heart.

9

DEATH IN THE MILKING PARLOUR

'Deckie' felt cheated. He was just twenty-four years of age, but already he had imagined the rest of his life: he and Bernie, the teenage lovers, would get married and her father would give them the farm. In his mind's eye he could see them walking side by side through the lush green pastures in the early morning to bring in the cattle for milking. It wasn't a big dream, but it was one that made Deckie happy.

But now the dream was turning into a nightmare. She was leaving him behind, going on courses and learning about things he had no time for. She was always busy, meeting new people and moving on in the world while he was content to stay here in this small rural backwater where he knew everybody and everybody knew him.

He used to trust her, but now he wasn't sure what was going on. He didn't want to believe it but he suspected she was seeing somebody behind his back.

He'd noticed a few of the lads smirking when he came into the pub. There had been some slagging about her getting off with one of his friends. But there was nothing he could get hold of. It was like trying to eat soup with a fork. He'd asked the other guy straight out, but he'd denied it to his face.

Deckie wasn't the brightest. He liked it when everything was plain and simple and there were no complications to confuse him. He was also drinking a lot and that wasn't helping things either. He'd got a bit maudlin and told his friends he wouldn't be around much longer. They didn't know what to make of him.

He'd never been one for the pubs until about a year ago when things first started to go badly between him and Bernie. Up to then he'd been happy to work the land in his spare time or just hang around her house, chatting about this and that. But lately he seemed to be in the pub half the time.

What hurt him most was that on her special night she hadn't even phoned him. That was when he'd got this awful feeling in the pit of his stomach that it was all coming out badly. That was when he began thinking he'd been cheated and that's when he began to see life through a long white tunnel of despair. In the space of four days he began to finally realise that he was losing Bernie.

Deckie felt cheated all right, in love and in life. Suddenly his dreams of the future were falling apart and the love he felt for Bernie becoming twisted by the fear of seeing the future he had mapped out for himself sink like a stone in a slurry pit.

They had first met on the school bus. Bernadette O'Neill was a teenage schoolgirl going to the Mercy Convent in Trim, Co Meath and Declan Lee was two years older and attending the nearby Christian Brothers school in the town.

They only lived about a mile apart, but there was a much

greater social gulf between the two families. Declan Lee was the third child in a family of five born to working-class couple Thomas and Monica Lee, who lived in a neat bungalow in Galtrim, near Summerhill, Co Meath. Declan was tall and thin and even in his early twenties he was baby faced and looked much younger than his years.

About a mile away Peter and Mary O'Neill lived on a lush fifty-acre farm at Freffans, between the village of Summerhill and the town of Trim. When they got married the O'Neills were told by their doctor that they couldn't have children, but Bernadette was their first miracle and a couple of years later a second daughter, Michelle, was born.

Bernadette was a good-looking and bright girl who enjoyed life. But she also had her father's ambition and determination to get on in the world.

Declan had failed his Intermediate Examination and left school at sixteen. He'd had a few odd jobs, helping on a milk round, working in a garage for a while, and he'd done a bit of labouring. But he didn't stick at anything, leading a fairly aimless existence until he was employed as a farm hand by Peter O'Neill.

It was a tough life, up early, hard work and the pay wasn't great. But he liked it because it was simple and it was the kind of life he knew about. He was good humoured and good company and Bernadette, who was sixteen at the time, fell for her father's slim, good-looking farm hand. They knew each other to see from the school bus and about a year after he came to work on their bustling farm where they were thrown together day and night Bernadette and Declan Lee started going out with each other.

'He had the run of the place,' said Bernie's mother, Mary.

She washed his clothes, gave him dinner and there was always a place at the table or a seat by the yellow Stanley range when Deckie came in from the fields.

In some ways he was more than just a farm hand. When he started going out with the O'Neill's eldest daughter he was almost welcomed into the family.

'He was the son I never had,' Mary O'Neill used to say when people remarked what a great help Declan was around the place. If there was a touch of sarcasm in her voice it was nothing to the bitterness that was to come.

Declan Lee always felt Bernadette's mother hadn't much time for him. He believed she looked down on him because he wasn't a farmer. Bernie's father was different. Like Declan he was a quiet man and they got on well together. They had the farming and the football in common.

A quiet and determined farmer, Peter O'Neill had built the family twenty-acre Land Commission smallholding into a fifty-acre dairy farm, no mean feat in Meath where land was expensive and hard to acquire. Bernadette had always helped around the place and as she turned from girl to woman she began to take charge of the farm while he was away.

When she finished school she got a job with the Dublin & District Milk Board recording milk yields from dairy farmers. She travelled around the rural areas of the county meeting other farmers and looking around their holdings. She was a smart girl and she was getting ideas and advice for the O'Neills' own farm.

Soon she took over the running of the place, supervising the building of a milking parlour and a cold storage area. Bernadette had great plans for expanding and she embarked on a one year 'Green Card' course with Teagasc, the farm-training organisation at Warrenstown Agricultural College, to learn farm management.

Of course Peter kept an eye on things, but he started buying and selling cattle and got involved in the cattle haulage side of the business. He was away a lot and more and more it was left to Bernadette and Declan to look after the place.

The couple had been going out together for four years when, in June 1993, they got engaged to be married. Declan had saved up for the ruby ring and twenty-one-year-old Bernadette showed it off proudly.

They opened a joint account in Trim Credit Union, they bought a green Toyota Corolla car together and they had joint insurance. They spent the summer holiday together, driving around Kerry and Clare. They enjoyed the break, at ease with one another and casting a professional eye over the land and the farms they passed through on their travels.

They were almost the ideal couple, a bit young perhaps but well used to one another because they spent so much time in each other's company, whether it was working or socialising. After the engagement the couple went househunting.

'We were like husband and wife,' according to Declan Lee.

But it was considered a bit unseemly for Declan the farm

hand to be engaged to the farmer's daughter. Nothing was said directly, but he got this feeling that the O'Neill's thought their daughter could do better for herself.

Bernadette's mother Mary, who loved her daughter dearly, was a bit cynical about the romance and her prospective son-in-law's character.

'There's no such thing as love,' she told him once and they exchanged words about his lack of drive and ambition.

But Declan was in love with Bernadette and he couldn't see any life beyond his life with her.

The reality was that Mary O'Neill didn't like him but she tolerated him for her daughter's sake. She knew he wasn't very intelligent but, worse, she saw a cruel streak in her future son-in-law. It frightened her to see him raise his gun expertly to his shoulder and kill rabbits and small birds without any qualms. She had even seen him shoot the half-wild kittens that scampered around the yard. He did it with a cold, calculating eye and without remorse.

'He'd shoot anything with life,' she said.

To ease the tension of always being around the place, and so that he would no longer be known as 'the hired help' Declan got a job with Meath County Council, weighing lorries of sand and gravel coming in to the council yard. The money was good, the hours were short and Declan had plenty of time to work on the farm, 'voluntarily'. That was different from just being another ordinary farm hand. It was giving him a stake in the place. Or so he thought. His expectation, especially after their engagement, was that the farm would be handed over to Bernie and himself when they got married.

At the weekends they might go shooting with a gang of friends, or watch a football match on a Sunday afternoon. Later they would adjourn to the pub and the crack was always good.

There was a large, happy group and among them was a good-looking eighteen-year-old teenager called Damien Dixon who was one of the gang. One night during the heady excitement of the 1994 World Cup, Bernadette O'Neill stumbled into him while the others were glued to a match. There was a bit of banter in a dark corner of the dancehall afterwards and they ended up kissing, tentatively at first and then with passionate intensity.

Suddenly Declan Lee didn't seem quite as important to Bernadette any more. Her new young man had reawakened the life in her. She had been with Declan Lee since she was an inexperienced seventeen-year-old girl. Now she realised that they were, as he said, like an old married couple and she had hardly lived at all.

Bernadette wanted to be free. She was meeting new people all the time, but Declan was stuck in a rut with the same crowd. He hadn't moved on since he'd failed his exams at school and slowly it dawned on her that he would never amount to much.

She knew Declan trusted her and she didn't like carrying on this clandestine relationship with one of his friends but there was no going back now. There was the added complication that Declan had built up his expectations about 'falling in' for the O'Neills' farm when he married her. In his mind there was no doubt that this was going to be his reward, not only for loving Bernadette, but for all the hard work he had done around the place.

Bernadette persuaded Declan that they needed a 'cooling off' period. She knew he had to be handled carefully, she had seen his temper flare and it wasn't a pretty sight. She just felt lucky she had never been on the receiving end of it. She didn't tell him that she had been seeing Damien Dixon on and off since June.

That summer of 1994, before they decided to take a break in their relationship, she and Declan had booked a holiday in Cyprus for September. Now, rather than let the tickets go to waste they went away together anyway. They enjoyed themselves, but it wasn't the same any more.

Still Declan couldn't see it. As far as he was concerned Bernadette was his lover and he was going to marry her. She was what made his life worthwhile. He wasn't about to let that go easily.

The Sunday after they got home from holidays Declan Lee went to a local GAA match and was surprised to see Bernadette already there with Damien Dixon. He had heard rumours about them.

'Is there something going on here that I don't know about?' he asked Dixon later.

'No!' replied the other young man, emphatically.

Declan Lee believed him, but he was uneasy.

Two weeks later, Friday October 7, was a big day for

Bernadette. Her proud mother and father and her younger sister Michelle were all at Warrenstown Agricultural College to see her presented with her 'Green Cert' as a trainee farmer. Afterwards they had a meal together and later that evening Bernadette told them she was going out, but didn't say where she was going or with whom.

She had arranged to meet her fiancé Declan in a pub in Navan but instead she phoned Damien Dixon. They met in a different bar in the town. Although it was her big day Bernadette was jumpy and nervous that night.

'We won't stay. Deckie is coming in to town. Let's go to Dunshaughlin,' she said to Dixon.

He wasn't fussy and he certainly didn't want a confrontation with her boyfriend. So they left that pub and drove to the nearby village where they were less likely to bump into people they knew.

While they were enjoying a close encounter in the car Declan Lee was sitting on a barstool in the pub in Navan, waiting for Bernadette. But she never came or contacted him to tell him why she wouldn't be there to celebrate the big occasion with him. It seemed that she had run out of excuses and she couldn't find the words to tell Declan that she didn't love him any more.

The following evening, Saturday, the crowd gathered in Jack Quinn's pub outside Trim. Bernadette and Declan and Damien were in the party. They went on a bit of a pub-crawl through the countryside. Declan asked her where she had been the previous evening and she made some half-hearted excuse. She was getting fed up with him pestering her all the time. She just wanted it to be over, but she didn't know how to tell him.

Declan Lee was in a funny mood that night. 'Where would you get a priest?' he asked at one stage.

Nobody really knew what he was talking about. He had a fair amount to drink so they didn't think much about it at the time.

They ended up at a dance in the Wellington Park Hotel in Trim. Declan Lee and Damien Dixon sat outside in the car while the rest of them tumbled in to the dance.

'You might as well come in, it's the last time you are going to see me,' Lee said to his love rival Dixon. 'Wait till you see, I won't be around any more,' he added.

When the dance was over Declan pleaded with Bernadette to bring him home in their car. He was very drunk and she agreed, reluctantly. He sat in and they began to argue. They didn't often argue, but tonight was different. Suddenly he turned vicious. She had never seen anything like it in her young life. He grabbed her, putting his two hands around her neck and began to tighten his grip. Her gold chain flew apart as she fought back and only because he was very drunk was she able to get him off her. But she was desperately frightened.

She threw him out of the car and drove home. It was 4 a.m. and she was distraught. But there was nobody she could really talk too.

Before she went to Mass the following morning she went

into the kitchen and had a cup of tea.

'I wish I was dead,' she told her mother with frightening suddenness.

Mary O'Neill was shocked when Bernadette related what Declan had done.

'You better speak to your father, he'll be able to do something,' she said. But they didn't really have time to discuss it before leaving the house to go to the village church.

Declan Lee was in his usual spot in the porch of the big grey church in Freffens. He rarely ventured into the body of the church itself, preferring to stand at the very back where it was easy to escape once Communion was called. He was waiting for her when she came out after the Mass. Bernadette was still livid about what had happened the previous night but she didn't want to make a scene in front of friends and neighbours who stood outside in the autumn sunshine chatting after the ceremony.

They had a brief and sullen conversation. He asked her for money. She gave him some, but she didn't invite him back to the house for dinner, as she often did when things were going well between them.

After Mass he went drinking. During the day he met Damien Dixon briefly. He told Dixon he was 'very hungover' from the previous night but he hoped 'a cure' would sort him out. He didn't mention the row with Bernadette and they didn't talk about the smouldering feud between them.

Bernadette went home to her Sunday lunch. Later in the afternoon she rang Damien Dixon and they met again in the pub in Dunshaughlin. She told the young man what had happened the night before and said she was afraid of her life what Declan Lee might do. They talked for a while, and then she said she had to go home. She had to be up early in the morning. They went to a takeaway restaurant and Bernadette got a snackbox to bring home.

When she got to the farmhouse at about 9.30 p.m. that Sunday night her father, Peter, was sitting in an armchair watching *The Sunday Game* on the television. She waited until the programme was over and then she told him she was going to break it off with Declan Lee the following day. She asked if he could be there to lend his support because she didn't know what Declan Lee might do when she told him.

'He'll listen to you,' she said, 'and if not you'll have to knock some sense into him.'

She told him about the incident outside the hotel the previous night. She said she had made up her mind to end the engagement and she was going to split their savings, buy his share of the car and take him off the insurance.

Peter O'Neill couldn't believe what she was telling him. He thought he knew Declan Lee, had never imagined there was a violent side to the man he had spent so much time with on the farm. He was angry that Declan had treated his daughter this way and although he was a man of few words he intended to let him know exactly how he felt. Peter O'Neill told his daughter he would be back from Maynooth Mart at 5 p.m. the following evening and not to do anything until then.

As Bernadette was going to bed Declan Lee was drinking

the last of about fifteen pints of beer he had consumed that day. He had got a bit of a slagging about the 'troubles' he was having with Bernie.

'There's someone taking her out from under ye, no names mentioned,' said one of the boys.

'You'll have to get compensation, all the work you've put into the place,' quipped another.

They could be merciless sometimes, but it was regarded as harmless banter among a crowd of lads. They didn't realise just how hurtful it was to Declan Lee's bruised ego.

'I won't let it go handy anyway,' he said, referring to his 'claim' on the farm for all his unpaid work over the years. There was bravado in his voice, but it was courage from the drink rather than the heart.

Twice during the evening Declan Lee left his pub stool and phoned the O'Neills, asking for Bernadette. He was told she wasn't in.

Declan ended the night playing pool in their local which was between Trim and Freffans.

It was dark when Bernadette O'Neill rose from her bed at 6.30 a.m. She dressed quickly, putting on a boiler suit over her clothes to protect them from the dirt. Her father was just about to leave in the truck. He told her he would be back at five o'clock that evening; she could depend on that.

She had a quick cup of tea and went down the fields to get the cattle. It was a fine dry October morning. There was a cool breeze, but she could tell it was going to be a pleasant day on the farm.

As she came back up herding the cows the lights went on in the milking parlour. Suddenly Declan Lee emerged out of the gloom as the first rays of light began to reveal a clear blue sky.

Her mother crossed the yard and said 'good morning' to Bernadette, but she didn't reply.

'Good morning, Bernie, it's a nice morning,' Declan greeted her.

'What's fucking good about it?' she answered sharply, prodding the cows on into the milking parlour where the machines were already humming as they warmed up. 'Daddy is raging at what you did to me on Saturday night – I showed him the chain,' she said, angrily.

He started to mumble an apology and began to tie up some of the cows.

'You go to work, I'll finish the milking,' he said, trying to humour her and get back into her good books.

'You needn't bother,' she answered.

He began to speak, but again she cut him off.

'I want you to leave, Deckie, because if my father comes back and catches you here he's going to kill you. I want you to leave now or I'm going to get the guards. I'm going to the credit union today and I'm going to split the money between us.'

He looked at her, stunned.

'Bernie, don't, please don't do this to me, I love you.'

He went over to give her a hug. But she pushed him away.

'Don't touch me, Deckie, I'm breaking it off with you.'

'You can't do this,' he pleaded.

'It's too late, I'm seeing Damien Dixon.'

It was as though she had taken a gun and shot him.

Declan Lee fled out of the milking parlour. For a moment she thought he was gone for good. She was relieved. Finally it was done.

But it wasn't over yet, not by a long shot.

Suddenly he came running back into the shed, but this time he was waving his double-barrelled shotgun. He couldn't see the cows now or hear the sucking sounds of the milking machines lined against the walls. All he could see was the love of his life, Bernadette, standing there between the rows of machines all alone as if he was looking at her down a 'long white tunnel'.

'Bernie, I love you. I can't live without you. We're both going to die here in this place,' he screamed.

He was standing about seven feet away from her when he raised the gun expertly to his shoulder. She looked at him, not believing he was capable of this. He thought he saw a smirk on her face. Then he opened fire.

The blast of the shotgun tore into her chest. About sixty pellets entered her body sending it into spasm and shock. But she was a tough girl, she didn't go down even though she had taken the brunt of the shotgun cartridge at such close range. Mortally wounded Bernadette let out a screech and stumbled towards him. He turned and fled.

As Declan Lee emerged into the beautiful blue dawn he found himself confronted by Bernadette's mother.

'Don't, Deckie!' Mary O'Neill shouted, seeing him raise

the shotgun a second time. As she did she stumbled and fell in the yard. He fired the gun at Mary and the shot exploded around her, but she wasn't hit. In a blind panic she rose and raced for the kitchen. She slammed the door and grabbed the telephone. She dialled 999 looking out the window into the yard.

'What's happening?' her younger daughter Michelle called from the bedroom after hearing the two loud bangs and the screaming in the yard. She ran into the kitchen.

Declan Lee went back to the milking parlour and looked in the window. The cows were milling around with the noise of the shooting. Bernadette O'Neill, the girl he'd loved and lost, was lying on her back in the walkway, stone dead.

Declan reached into the pocket of the green sleeveless hunting jacket he was wearing. He fumbled about until he found a long red cartridge. He turned and looked towards the house. The light was still on in the kitchen and he could see Mary O'Neill talking frantically on the telephone.

He broke open the gun and expertly slotted the deadly cartridge into the chamber.

'I'm doing this for Bernie,' he shouted.

He pressed the barrel of the gun close to his heart. He reached down to the trigger and pulled.

He even heard the bang. The impact blew him five or six feet across the farmyard where he lay in the mud with a gaping hole in his chest.

This is it now, I'm going to join Bernie, he thought, as he hovered between life and death. He was unconscious for a few moments and then he woke up again. He knew he was still lying in the farmyard in the October dawn. I'm a spirit, he thought in the eerie silence. I'm some sort of spirit that cannot die.

Declan Lee was right. He didn't die. The self-inflicted gunshot caused horrific injuries, including the loss of one of his lungs, but he survived. When he got out of hospital he was charged with the murder of Bernadette O'Neill. A jury found him not guilty of murder, but guilty of manslaughter. He was sentenced to four years in prison.

It was like a hammer blow to Mary O'Neill. Her daughter was dead, yet within a few short years Declan Lee was back in the parish picking up the threads of his previous life.

My daughter Michelle bumped into him on New Year's Eve and I said to her, 'Did you shout "Killer! You killer! You killed my sister!" across the dance floor?' But she said she just froze. I would have done something. I don't know what, but I would have done something.

10
CALL YOURSELF A MAN?

There was never any doubt about who killed the twenty-one-year-old vivacious blonde, Valerie Lenihan. Her lover walked into the police station and gave himself up.

It was 3.05 a.m. on the first Sunday of December, 1994, when Gerry Mullane marched up to the desk in Anglesea Street Garda station in Cork and announced to Garda John Leahy in a calm and steady voice, 'Jesus, I need help. I've stabbed my girlfriend. I might have killed her.'

It turned out to be something of an understatement. Poor naked Valerie Lenihan, the girl whose mother said she 'looked like a film star' when she left for a date that evening, never had a chance. He had strangled her with such force that blood vessels in her eyes had burst from the pressure of his vice-like grip on her throat. Then he'd plunged a kitchen knife into her chest – twice.

The first wound was four inches long and passed through her eighth rib, her diaphragm and liver before penetrating her stomach. The second stab wound was inflicted with such force that it went right through her body, coming out her back. The sharp blade sliced through her left lung and then cut the aorta, the main artery to the heart.

Gerry Mullane then washed the blood off his hands and arms and went for a walk.

'I went to get help,' he explained later.

But it took him over an hour to make the short journey from his flat to the police station. Mullane insisted that his girlfriend was 'still breathing' when he left the flat, but all the evidence would suggest that this could not possibly be true.

So why did the thirty-three-year-old once married man murder his beautiful twenty-one-year-old lover in such a brutal and bloody fashion? If he believed she was still breathing when he fled from the room why did he leave her naked on the bed to bleed to death?

He came up with a great story. Everyone wanted to believe it because it carried such conviction. But it portrayed his young lover as a terrible bitch who had raged at him because he couldn't get a 'hard-on' when she was desperate for sex.

Was Gerry Mullane telling the truth? Or had he spent well over an hour on a cold December morning concocting a story that would explain his rage yet elicit as much sympathy as anyone who callously carves up his lover could possibly get?

Gerry Mullane was a gas fitter from Emly, Co Tipperary, who had come to work as a contractor connecting up the natural gas system to customers in Cork city in June of 1992. He had been married and was the father of two children. One child had died of a cot death putting a great deal of strain on his marriage. He was now separated and living in a one-bedroom flat in McCurtain Street in the centre of the city.

He met twenty-one-year-old Valerie Lenihan, from Kiltalla

Gardens in Knocknaheeney, in a night club about seven months before he killed her. Valerie's parents had been separated since she was nine years of age and she still lived at home with her mother, Carmel.

'Gerry the Gas', as he was known, and Valerie got on well together, although friends described the relationship as 'stormy'. During the week Valerie stayed with her mother and at weekends she stayed over with her lover in the city. After a couple of months they decided that she would move in to his flat after Christmas.

Valerie didn't have a lot of money, but she loved beautiful things. She had a fabulous figure and she wore the clothes to show it off. Any money she had left over she spent on make-up and perfume and jewellery. She also lavished money on the hairdresser who kept her long blonde hair in the latest fashionable style.

About seven weeks before she was murdered Valerie came into town on a Friday night. She met Gerry in the pub and told him she was pregnant.

'She wasn't too pleased at first, but as time passed she got happier about it,' said Gerry later. He wasn't all that pleased either. He hadn't left one set of family responsibilities to get involved with another.

'I think I'd look after her and support her,' he had said half-heartedly when asked what his intentions were.

But in the end it didn't arise. Fate intervened to get him off the hook before he had to make a real commitment. On Monday night, November 28, 1994, Valerie arrived at the flat unexpectedly. Gerry brought her in, surprised to see her.

'I've had a miscarriage,' she told him. She had been pregnant for about two months and had only told her mother the news earlier that day.

Gerry didn't say anything. He just put his arms around her and the two of them stood like that for a very long time, mourning for the loss of a child they would never have. Ironically it was the beginning of the week that would turn out to be Valerie's last.

She was a strong-willed and demanding girl. She was what might be called 'high maintenance' in that she expected to be treated like a lady. She wasn't only demanding in terms of money, she was also very demanding when it came to sex. At least that's the way Gerry Mullane portrayed his lover.

The first few months had been great for Gerry but lately he was beginning to feel the pressure. She was a young woman who liked dressing up and going to nice places. She liked crowded bars, cool night clubs and staying out late with her younger friends. He was thirty-three and been through all that before and now he liked a few quiet pints. While he tried to please Valerie he didn't always succeed.

Valerie's father just didn't like him. He never had. On the other hand, her mother, Carmel, really did like him. She and Valerie were like sisters, rather than mother and daughter. They did everything together, going shopping and buying jewellery. They confided in each other, even about lovers. That week the two of them had gone shopping. It was the first week in December and after hours traipsing around the shops

Valerie had come home with her Christmas outfit.

Little did Valerie know that instead of wearing it to Mass on Christmas morning she would be wearing her new outfit when she was laid out in a coffin for her own funeral Mass.

On Saturday, December 3, Gerry Mullane got up at about 6.45 a.m. and he was on the job at 7 a.m. He had a hard day and by 3.30 that afternoon when the work was done he had worked up a thirst that only a couple of pints could quench. He had agreed to meet Valerie in their local at 8.30 p.m. that night, so himself and a few mates adjourned to a nearby pub. He wasn't able to say exactly how much he drank but it was between three and five pints of lager.

As he was sitting in the pub Valerie was dolling herself up, as she always did, for the night out. She liked to look her best, even if they were just going to the local for a few drinks.

'See you in the morning,' she called to her mother as she left the house to get the bus into the city centre. When she got to the pub Gerry wasn't there, so she ordered herself a drink and waited.

She didn't like it when he did this to her. It showed a lack of respect and it meant he was putting something else before her. Valerie wasn't the kind of girl who took kindly to that sort of treatment.

He was about fifteen minutes late and she knew by him that he already had a skinful. It was the usual conversation between couples when this happens.

'How many did you have?'

'Two.'

'You bloody liar, you've had at least four!'

But she mellowed after a while and they had six or seven pints each by closing time. They weren't fit to go on anywhere so they decided to go back to the flat, which was on the third floor of a building in McCurtain Street. When they got in the door he opened a couple of cans and they began to get amorous.

They went into the bedroom and stripped off. The two of them were sitting on the bed naked when the argument started. It was one of those stupid arguments that have no real meaning, just two people worse for drink hitting off each other.

'If you were man enough I'd still be pregnant,' Valerie taunted him, talking about the miscarriage.

'What do you fucking mean by that?' he asked.

'You probably haven't got enough sperm in you!' she answered.

One insult led to another, each taunt to a reprisal. They kept it up for thirty minutes, arguing back and forth and blaming each other for problems in their relationship.

It got so loud that Catherine Bulman who was sleeping in the apartment underneath woke up with the noise. When she looked at the bedside clock it was 1.20 a.m.

Gerry and Valerie finished off a couple of cans each and they got under the covers. It was now well into Sunday morning. They were both drunk, but Gerry Mullane was drunk and tired, he just wanted to lay his head on the pillow and go to sleep. However Valerie wanted more. She rolled over on top of him and began to urge him to have sex with her.

They tried to make love but as they fumbled towards sex he just couldn't get an erection. He couldn't perform. It had never happened to him before but the combination of tiredness and drink had left him limp and ashamed.

'You're drunk . . . again,' Valerie reproached him as he struggled to focus on fulfilling her wishes. 'You call yourself a fucking man? You're on about trying for a child again and you can't even get a hard-on,' she continued.

'Would you leave it out and give me a fucking break!' he replied, anger in his voice.

Inside he was raging with himself but powerless to do anything about it. He leaped from the bed and ran across the twenty-four feet to the kitchen hatch where he snatched a carving knife from the counter. He ran back towards her, holding the gleaming blade aloft.

'I'll fucking kill you!' he roared.

'You would, would you?' she taunted him again.

Suddenly he threw her back on the bed and plunged the blade into her chest. Then he raised his arm and struck again.

Appalled at what he had done, he washed the blood from his hands and arms and dressed quickly and ran from the room. Valerie was still alive when he slammed the door.

At least that's the way Gerry Mullane told the story to the police.

'If I hadn't come in here I'd have killed myself,' he told detectives who listened to his tale of woe in the early hours of that Sunday morning.

But it was a story that never really hung together properly. Not that it made any difference – it didn't save him from a life sentence. But it did give him some vague sort of self-justification for a horrendous crime. It was as if he had an excuse for what he had done. Having one's manhood insulted by a young woman is something that would bring out the passion in any red-blooded male. It would almost make you reach for the carving knife!

'I just completely flipped,' explained Gerry Mullane. 'The next thing I knew we were struggling on the bed. I realised I was after stabbing Valerie.'

His story also gave the impression that it was a spur of the moment thing, a crime of rage and passion. But could it have been a far more calculated act than he was prepared to admit?

There was something about Gerry Mullane that wasn't obvious to everybody, but it certainly made an impression on Valerie's father, Tom, even though he had only met Mullane on a couple of occasions.

'I never liked Mullane. I didn't want him as a son-in-law. I'm sharp, but I couldn't put my finger on why I didn't like him. For a start he didn't look you in the eye when he talked to you.'

But even more importantly he claimed that Valerie had been trying to break it off with her older lover for about four weeks before she was murdered.

'He just wouldn't accept it. He was obsessed with her and

I heard him threaten that he would do time for her,' said Tom Lenihan. 'When I heard this I begged her to tell me where he lived so I could deal with him, but she wouldn't because she didn't want me to get into trouble.'

So the question remains: was the killing of Valerie Lenihan premeditated, rather than the drunken, frenzied attack her killer claimed took place? He was never able to explain how and why he had choked Valerie. The story he gave was implausible.

'I think I caught her by the throat once or twice and pushed her away,' he said, claiming that this had happened during the heated argument before the actual stabbing and murder of Valerie.

When pressed to explain her injuries he said he had no recollection of strangling her. But Valerie had been gripped so tightly that blood vessels in her eyes had burst and her neck was severely bruised. It would have taken at least half a minute of constant pressure to do the damage that he inflicted – before he set about her with the knife.

In another crucial piece of evidence Catherine Bulman, the girl in the flat downstairs, said she distinctly heard Valerie crying during the prolonged argument. It doesn't sound like the sexually voracious woman that Mullane portrayed in his evidence.

But probably the most damning piece of evidence to discredit Gerry Mullane's story was given by forensic psychiatrist Dr Jennifer Ryan: there was semen in the vaginal swabs taken from Valerie Lenihan during the post mortem. If

Gerry Mullane couldn't get 'a hard on' as he maintained, how could Valerie Lenihan have had sex?

Could it be that between 1.20 a.m. and 3.05 a.m. that December Sunday morning as he walked the cold streets of Cork Gerry Mullane had invented a story to cover the calculated and clinical killing of his young lover? By portraying himself as a wronged male he might win the hearts of a jury who would treat the killing of a young woman as a crime of passion, rather than a cold-blooded murder borne out of jealousy and hatred because she was going to dump him for someone younger.

Gerry Mullane's first conviction was overturned and it was only after a second trial that he was given life in prison.

But even today his words ring hollow.

'I loved Valerie. I didn't want to do harm to her,' said the man who put a knife through her body with such force that it came out her back.

It was a strange kind of love.

11

THE MONSTER
IN THE GARAGE

It was dark and they should have been in bed, but their mam hadn't come home and their dad had let them stay up late. Daddy seemed agitated since they'd arrived home from school that day and he kept going out, even after it got dark, leaving the eight-year-old girl to look after her two brothers, aged five and three, and the baby. He said he was looking for their mam, but each time he came back and said, 'No luck.'

The three-year-old boy was in his pyjamas but he was too hyped-up to sleep. He went in to the others, his voice filled with wonder and excitement.

'There's a monster in the garage,' he blurted out. Their father had gone out again so the three of them, the eight-year-old girl and the two boys, stole from their beds and went downstairs. The girl switched off the burglar alarm and they all went into the garage. They could see something lying in the darkness and the little boy went right up and asked the 'monster' a question.

'But she didn't answer me,' he remembered.

Then suddenly the light went on and their dad was standing in the doorway.

Aware of Swamp Monsters and other scary creatures the little boy tried to bolt for the safety of his bedroom, but his father was blocking the way. The man took the three-year-old by the hand and told them all to go upstairs to bed. Then he slapped them.

In the morning, before she went to school, his daughter asked him about it.

'What was that in the garage last night?'

'It was just a monster,' he said, borrowing his little son's description of what they had seen.

Within an hour of the conversation his wife and their mother, Patricia Murphy, was found lying dead in her underwear beside a builder's skip about 170 metres away from the house on Dublin's northside where they lived. She had been hit over the head with a hammer and strangled with a belt.

The children put the incident of the 'monster in the garage' out of their minds. When they were asked about the day their mother disappeared they said nothing about their secret trip to the garage in the dead of night.

At the funeral David Murphy looked out of place in a beige jacket over a white shirt and black tie. Tall and thin, the expression on his face was one of incomprehension. Looking at the coffin of his murdered wife leaving the church he appeared to be saying to himself what all husbands must say on such occasions: 'How can this be happening to me?' He held a distraught old woman by the right arm, as though keeping her from collapsing with grief on the church steps.

She was his elderly mother-in-law, Bridget 'Biddy' Behan, witnessing her beloved daughter's last journey from church to grave. His concern seems as palpable as her grief.

They hated each other.

David Murphy was always an oddball and a loner. He grew up in Dublin but when he arrived at the Atlantic Hotel in Kilkee, Co Clare, to install disco lights, it was as if he had appeared out of a mirage: he was alone, seemingly with no ties and no past. He was doing an electrician's work, but he wasn't an electrician. When the job was finished he never left. He simply stayed on, living in a room in the hotel until people found jobs for him to do and, almost without anybody realising it, he assumed the job of general handyman in the place.

David Murphy seemed, at the age of twenty-four, to be starting life all over again. He was always hanging on the edge of the crowd, always listening, but never drawing attention to himself, lulling those around him into thinking he almost didn't exist.

The only thing that seemed to really matter to David Murphy was to get money any way he could so that he could lose it. Kilkee held the fatal attraction of streets lined with amusement arcades and other dens where he could gamble and play the slot machines. Sometimes he earned the money, sometimes he stole it, sometimes he borrowed it. He really didn't care as long as he got his 'fix'. Whatever way he acquired the money, he soon lost it.

But until people got to know him really well they never

considered him a loser. Within days of arriving in the holiday town of Kilkee in May 1985 he met a local girl and they started going out together. There was a story that she became pregnant but it seems he just ditched her when somebody else came along.

He was odd but he had a manner that women found attractive. It was almost a false kind of politeness, ostentatiously holding the door open for a woman or fussing unnecessarily at the lift to allow other people in.

One night at a disco he was introduced to Patricia Behan who came from the town of Kilrush about eight miles away. He started going out with Patricia, telling her that he had finished with his other girlfriend. But Bridget Behan, Patricia's mother, wasn't so sure.

Biddy was forty-one when Patricia was born in London in October of 1962. Biddy already had another daughter, Christine, who was twenty and who had left home by the time her baby sister was born.

Soon after Patricia's birth, Biddy's husband disappeared and she returned with her daughter to her home town of Kilrush to live with her brother Kevin Danaher.

Patricia attended the local Convent of Mercy school. On leaving, Patricia worked in an ice cream factory before getting a job in the Orchard Hotel in the town. Like other girls her age she loved to dance and she and her friends used to get the bus to Kilkee to go to the disco in the Atlantic Hotel. In the winter of 1986, she met David Murphy.

David Murphy, just a few months older than herself, was

charming and convincing. Soon the two of them were going out together and within a few months they moved into a flat above the Educational Building Society office in Kilkee.

That Christmas Patricia had a miscarriage and the couple decided in the weeks that followed that they would get married. Biddy Behan was very unhappy about this turn of events – she was a dominant mother who needed attention and she had never liked the young Dubliner, resenting him because he had taken her daughter away from her. Besides, she had heard from friends tales about the pregnant girlfriend he had abandoned. But there was no talking to Patricia.

The bride wore a white wedding dress and he wore a black morning suit with a carnation in his buttonhole. There were twenty-five guests at the wedding reception on May 22, 1987, in the Orchard Hotel, where Patricia now worked as a housekeeper. But none of them, not even the best man, was a friend of David Murphy. They were all Patricia's family and friends. It was as if she was marrying a twenty-six-year-old orphan.

Almost immediately there was trouble in the relationship. If David was a gambler, Patricia was a drinker. The world seemed a much happier place after a few vodkas and Coke. Sometimes when Patricia had too much to drink he got very angry. One evening they had a ferocious row in the dining room of the Atlantic Hotel where he was doing a job. She had come in, tipsy, looking for him. As they tussled in the room she tripped over a table set for dinner, knocking it over and smashing the crockery. A waiter saw Murphy grab a butter knife in a fit of rage and lunge at Patricia – but he went no further when he realised he was being watched.

Patricia was under enormous pressure from her mother to return to Kilrush but David Murphy wanted to keep as far away from his mother-in-law as possible. He warned Patricia that he would go back to Dublin rather than move. But after their first child was born on April 16, 1988, he changed his tune. Patricia was having a difficult time living in a flat above an office and it was interfering with his life in the slot machine arcades, so he relented: they would move to Kilrush after all. Biddy Behan worked on contacts she had in the council and the young family got a new council house which adjoined her own 'Cosy Cottage' on Wilson Road. Now she could be close to her daughter.

'Pat's mother was a selfish woman. I never got on with her from the day I met her,' said David Murphy. 'We would be sitting there and her mother would be looking at me over her glasses.'

He didn't understand the close bond between mother and daughter. He and Patricia fought about the amount of time Patricia now spent in her mother's house, gossiping over cups of tea. The two women also ganged up on him about his previous relationship, claiming he was still seeing the woman. Aware of his gambling, Patricia began to hide money from him, encouraged by her mother,

After moving to Kilrush Murphy left the Atlantic Hotel and decided to go into business for himself, installing fitted kitchens and doing general handiwork. To customers he seemed like the ideal man for the job – he was cheap, considerate and nothing was ever too much trouble. He wasn't like the sneering tradesmen they were used too. But after people gave him money the work never seemed to get done. He disappeared with the cash into the arcades and played the slot machines with obsessive intensity. Then he would start borrowing from one person to buy material for another until his jobs were an unfinished mess. Everyone was unhappy, including his mother-in-law who had to listen to complaints from neighbours and friends to whom she had recommended him.

He would hide in the back room when people called to the house, leaving his wife to try to mollify irate customers. Like all cowards David Murphy was afraid of the strong and the assertive, but would take out his anger and frustration on his wife, beating her in his rages.

Nothing seemed to work for him, but he was always optimistic that one day it would all turn out for the best. He sold industrial sewing machines, he worked for a sign company travelling around Limerick, Clare and Galway and then he spent months installing lights in dancehalls and hotel ballrooms around the west of Ireland.

But all the time the debts were mounting – and David Murphy was now borrowing to feed his gambling habit. Patricia was also drinking heavily, although she eased up after their first child.

'Pat started coughing up blood, so she gave up the hard stuff,' explained her husband.

Patricia had insisted on one smart move. When the local council introduced a tenant purchase scheme she had insisted that they buy the house. She took out a loan and got some help from her mother to do so. Murphy persuaded her to take out a further £2,000 loan from the credit union to do an extension but this he blew on slot machines and other useless pursuits.

They decided to leave Kilrush for Dublin in September 1994 by which time the Murphys had few friends, debts of more than £9,000 with the local credit union and three small children.

David Murphy looked forward to going home to Dublin's northside. But Patricia wasn't so happy; she said she'd give it a year. Biddy Behan was distraught.

David Murphy was glad to get the feel of the city streets under his feet again after eight years in the wilderness of Co Clare. He had been brought up in Munster Street, Phibsboro on the north side of the city, and had left the local Christian Brothers school just a few weeks after a failed Intermediate Certificate. Although he had been thrown out of his father's house in a fit of temper, after which he torched four cars on the road, he now reestablished contact with the family.

He rented a house in Griffith Avenue and the family moved in to start a new life in the city. He had a substantial sum of money from the sale of the Kilrush house, and he made sure to get it safely into his care before any of the restless creditors who were pursuing him could get their hands on it.

Although their marriage had been stormy, characterised by domestic violence, gambling and drinking, it also had its tender side. Patricia called him by the pet Irish name Daithí and he called her Collie. Patricia even had these names inscribed on a plate which she hung on her bedroom door.

Once settled, they had to invite Biddy Behan to Dublin to visit and this led to further conflict and tension in the marriage. In all, she came five times to visit. Each time Patricia had to go down to Clare on the bus to collect her and bring her back to Dublin and then when the visit was over do the journey in reverse. It infuriated David Murphy and ruined their first Christmas in Dublin.

'She has the free travel, why the fuck can't she just get on the bus and come up on her own and you can meet her in Dublin?' he raged.

Heavily pregnant with their fourth child Patricia travelled all the way by bus to Kilrush and accompanied her mother back to Dublin. On Christmas Eve they arrived back at Griffith Avenue. Everything was ready for the Christmas visit but David Murphy was still livid about his mother-in-law's demanding ways and went to a gambling arcade. He lost all his money, but worse, in his wife's eyes, he didn't bother to buy a Christmas card for his mother-in-law. In such small details great rows are made.

They raged and ranted at each other all through Christmas Day and St Stephen's Day until everyone was exhausted, and yet neither of them would give in.

'She was in the bedroom all Christmas day and you could

see she'd been crying. Her eyes were all swollen,' reported Biddy Behan who couldn't wait to get out of the house and back home to Co Clare.

'It was much ado about nothing,' said Murphy nonchalantly.

David Murphy was getting odd jobs installing en-suite bathrooms and such like, although he was now even more feckless than before and could never seem to finish anything. He was also drawing £152 a week dole. The family paid £33 a week in rent, with the Eastern Health Board paying the balance of £91. But they were already in arrears with their rent.

Despite mounting debts Murphy was able to find money for one little extra, apart from his gambling. He paid £17 to an insurance broker for various policies – including one on the life of his wife.

After arriving in Dublin Patricia got a job in a bakery in the Omni Park centre in Santry, north Dublin. In mid-July £2000 went mysteriously missing from the shop. Investigations revealed that David Murphy had a duplicate key. Both he and Patricia were arrested and he was convicted of theft and given the Probation Act. Patricia was fired.

Their fourth child, a girl, was born the following year on January 11, 1996. Patricia soon slimmed down to an attractive size twelve but whether the weight loss was caused by tension and arguments or because she was trying to woo the man she loved all over again after nine years of a turbulent marriage it was hard to say.

Their life was in a mess: the landlord wanted his money, David Murphy couldn't keep up with the jobs he'd taken on, Patricia was agitating to go back to Clare, and the four children needed constant attention and care.

'She can go back but I won't be going back and neither will the kids,' David Murphy told one of the neighbours.

Something had to give.

Biddy Behan's last time to see her daughter came when her eldest grandchild made her First Holy Communion. As usual Patricia had to travel down to Kilrush to collect her mother, bring her to Dublin for the big day and bring her home again the following day.

Biddy Behan hadn't wanted to give the Communion money directly to the child in case David Murphy got his hands on it, so she had sent the money order for £150 to Patricia before the Communion so that she could buy a few things for herself and the child. But David Murphy managed to intercept it, and cashed it. He also took some of the £200 Communion money his daughter collected from friends and neighbours.

To try to fend off eviction from Griffith Avenue, Patricia Murphy was now working in Lismore House, a B&B in Drumcondra, ten or fifteen minutes' walk from the house. On the morning of Monday, May 27, 1996, she kissed the children goodbye and they waved her off at the door before 8 a.m. After breakfast David, who was now looking after the children, walked them up the road to the school at the bottom of Valentia Road. He was wheeling the baby in a buggy and their passage along the road was recorded by a camera at Drumcondra post office at 8.54 am. The buggy clearly had a tray under it at the time.

Worried about her baby daughter who had been sick that morning, Patricia served breakfast in the B&B and then shortly after 10 a.m. left early to go back to the house. She was last seen alive thirty houses away, walking briskly towards her own front door.

When Patricia arrived home David was there with the baby and the three-year-old boy.

'Take her to the doctor, please,' she pleaded.

'She's not sick, we don't have the money,' he answered. It was after 11 a.m. and as they argued they moved out the back door and into the garden.

At around midday a neighbour heard the three-year-old crying to be let into the house.

'I want to do a wee wee,' he cried. Eventually the door opened.

At about 2.30 p.m. David Murphy collected the children from school. When they got home their mother wasn't there as she usually was to make the lunch.

'We said we'd give her fifteen more minutes,' said the eldest girl. They waited and waited.

David Murphy left the house, leaving her in charge, but soon returned saying he couldn't find their mother. They all went out then, to walk around the nearby roads and search. Still nothing. They got home exhausted and went up to bed for a rest. Later they went out again.

The rest of the day and night was a blur but David Murphy left and returned at various times. Still their mother hadn't returned and so they all went to bed. It was then that the three-year-old revealed his secret to his older sister and brother, 'There's a monster in the garage.'

When David and Patricia Murphy had argued in the garden that morning, something snapped and he turned on her.

'Daddy hammered Mam on the head,' the three-year-old said later.

She fell down and he dragged her into the garage, closing the door behind him.

After slapping the children and putting them to bed David Murphy realised he had to do something. He lifted the prone body of his wife and put her in the buggy. He covered her over with a blanket and went out again, wheeling the stiffening corpse of the woman who had loved him along the dark, empty suburban street.

There was a builder's skip up a laneway at The Rise in Glasnevin, a stone's throw from the house. He toppled Patricia out onto the rough rubble lying beside it in the lane. As he did so, the tray underneath the buggy came loose.

It was after midnight when John Judd let his dog out for a run. He was standing leaning on the railings of his home when he heard a splash in the River Tolka. Instinctively he looked up and saw a man standing on the footbridge. Walking towards the bridge he saw a plastic bag floating in the water. As he approached, the man walked away and didn't look back.

At 1 a.m. David Murphy rang the gardaí and reported his wife missing. A squad car was sent around to the house and gardaí took the details.

At 4.30 a.m. Alan O'Loughlin was delivering milk along Griffith Avenue when he came across David Murphy. Murphy bought two litres of milk from him and told him to keep the change from £2.

The following morning, May 28, David Murphy telephoned Biddy Behan and asked her if she knew where Patricia was. However, he rang back later and said it was all right, she had stayed the night with a friend in Bray. But the elderly woman knew something was wrong.

Then a workman passing the skip in The Rise saw the nearly naked body of Patricia Murphy lying amid the rubble. She had been strangled, most likely by a belt wrapped around her neck and the noose tightened brutally so she could no longer breathe.

The hunt for a callous killer was on. David Murphy was the only suspect . . . and he knew it.

Detectives soon heard about the splash in the Tolka River. They found the plastic shopping bag and inside, soaked, was a multicoloured jacket, a pair of green jeans, a pink shirt, a trouser belt, a pair of socks and a child's hair comb. A friend, Eimer Lawlor, identified the jacket as belonging to Patricia. She said that the pink shirt and the green trousers were worn by David Murphy when she saw the family sheltering from the rain in Mobhi Road, Glasnevin on the Sunday afternoon before the murder. The tray of the buggy, which was missing, was found in another builder's skip some distance away.

After Patricia's murder, Murphy was rewarded for his conscientious insurance payments: the Royal Liver insurance company paid him £2,000 in funeral expenses and a lump sum of £8,000. It was more money than David Murphy ever had in his lifetime. But it didn't last. He soon got through it and had to work the streets of Dublin as a bicycle courier while detectives continued to try to pin the murder on him.

But nearly a year later and with his children taken into care, David Murphy began to believe that he had committed the perfect crime. There was nothing but circumstantial evidence against him. Now he claimed he was being hounded by the police.

'The bastards even brought me in and and showed me photographs of my dead wife,' he said. 'They think they are clever by doing all this, but they are not clever enough to catch me out.'

However, in March 1997 the two boys, who were now in a foster home, mentioned for the first time 'the monster in the garage'. About a month later the older girl also spoke about what went on in the house that night, the night her mother never came home and the children witnessed the dreadful sight in the garage. She was just that little bit older now and able to articulate what she couldn't say as an eight-year-old. The story the children told would send a chill through even the hardest heart. As they stood in the garage looking at the 'monster', their dad had suddenly appeared and switched on the light.

'When the light was on we could see our mam's body lying against the wall with her head sort of slanted like that,' said the little girl, tipping her own head to the right.

'Dad shouldn't have done that to Mam,' said the youngest boy to his foster mother.

'What?' she asked.

'He hit her with the hammer, the big one.'

'Where?'

'In the garden,' said the little boy. 'Mammy fell asleep and Daddy put Mammy in the garage.'

But as he spoke the older boy kept interrupting, 'Its all a dream, don't mind him.'

But then he too admitted he had seen 'this body lying on the floor' and although he was scared, he could remember a rope around his mother's neck.

With the evidence of his own children as well as circumstantial evidence about the state of the Murphys' marriage, detectives swooped on David Murphy. He was arrested on April 17, 1997, a month short of the first anniversary of the murder of his wife, Patricia.

David Murphy insisted to anyone who would listen that he had enjoyed 'a very good marriage'. 'We understood each other and we were good friends, but like all couples we did have the odd argument,' he said. 'But they were few and far between.'

By now nobody believed his lies.

'I had been telling them the truth all along – they just weren't listening to me,' he said and pointed out that his children hadn't said anything about the 'monster' when they first described what happened nearly a year earlier.

'I honestly don't know why my children said this,' he insisted.

'You very coldly and in cold blood murdered your wife and have come along here to brazen it out,' said prosecuting counsel Gregory Murphy SC.

'I didn't,' replied David Murphy.

But the jury were listening to the children. They didn't believe that the three fresh-faced children – who gave evidence by video link for the first time in the history of the Irish legal system – could have made up such a horrendous story as 'the monster in the garage'.

Just two days before his thirty-seventh birthday on Christmas Eve, David Murphy was convicted and sentenced to life in prison for the murder of his wife Patricia.

12

A WEDDING AND TWO FUNERALS

It was the night before the wedding and the beautiful young bride was staying with her parents at her grandmother's house in a small picturesque Irish village making the final preparations for her big day. About twenty miles away the groom's wedding eve party was in full swing in the hotel where he and his friends were staying for the night. There was drink at every table and the money was flying over the bar.

It was well past midnight and Michelle Taylor was hanging on every word John said. Young and sexy with long black hair and a taut, well-toned body, the twenty-year-old Londoner was obsessively in love with John. Her problem was that he was about to get married in the morning to somebody else. But throughout his engagement he had never stopped having sex with her. He told her that night, on the eve of his wedding, he couldn't really see any reason why that should change.

As the laughter spread around the hotel bar she wondered ruefully why she had come all this way from her home in London to see the 'Irish charmer' who had stolen her virginity walk down the aisle. But there was just something about the handsome devil she couldn't resist. Tall with slicked-back black hair like an old-style Hollywood movie actor he was perfectly dressed and cut a dashing figure no matter where he went. How she hated his beautiful twenty-year-old bride-to-be, Alison, the person she had already described in her secret diary as an 'unwashed bitch'.

Michelle wasn't the only one who was losing a lover in the morning. Earlier in the night another of his conquests begged him to call the wedding off. John Shaughnessy, with his cool, laconic Irish accent that melted women's hearts and broke their reserve, just laughed.

Michelle Taylor was staying in a bed and breakfast with other friends of the couple who had travelled over from London for the wedding. John had invited her as a guest of both Alison and himself, but she knew it was really John who wanted her there. He had paid for everything, without telling Alison, and insisted that she should drive over with them from London in the hired car. When the custom that the bride should not see her intended husband on the eve of the marriage had been invoked, Michelle got a call at the B&B where she was staying.

'Why don't you stay the night in the hotel? It will be good crack and there's a spare room just down the corridor from my own,' he said.

She just knew there was a twinkle in his eye as he said it. She didn't need to be asked twice: she gathered a few things and he collected her in the car. Later that night when most of the other guests had gone to bed they staggered up the stairs.

He went to his room, she went to hers. It was around 3 a.m. and she had only thrown off her shoes when the phone rang. She knew it would.

'Have you got any tea?' he asked with a laugh. 'I'm in the mood for a cup of tea.'

'How about a spot of flower arranging?' she replied.

It was their little joke, their code word. And it was what they usually did on Monday nights.

Michelle could never say no and a few minutes later she tiptoed across the corridor and into John's room.

As Alison Blackmore lay asleep dreaming of her perfect wedding the following morning, her tall, handsome husband-to-be, John Shaughnessy, lay naked under the covers in his hotel bedroom making love until dawn with Michelle Taylor, the girl who helped him with his flower arrangements.

Bobby and Breda Blackmore had moved to London from the village of Piltown, Co Kilkenny when they married. The couple had four children, Alison being the second eldest. Every summer Alison stayed with her grandmother in Ireland and when it came to making her First Holy Communion she returned to Piltown rather than receive the sacrament in London.

Alison was 'quiet, shy and trusting' but as she grew into a beautiful young girl she was much admired when she came back home to her parents' Kilkenny village. She loved the Irish way of life, the pubs, the chat and the friendships. When she was just sixteen and finished her convent education,

Alison started hanging around an Irish haunt in north London, the Archway Tavern. It was there one night in October 1986 that she bumped into handsome, sweet-talking John Shaughnessy from the village of Ballintubber, Co Roscommon.

Shaughnessy had finished his education at the local vocational education college and had been over and back to England for a few years doing odd jobs. Twenty-four-year-old Shaughnessy had just started a new job as a porter in a well-known private hospital in south London, the Churchill Clinic in Lambeth Road. In another part of the building Michelle Taylor had also just started a new job as an accounts clerk.

Shaughnessy, who stayed in a room at the staff hostel beside the clinic at 60–62 Lambeth Road, started going out with the young Alison Blackmore. Since she lived north of the city he tended to socialise at the Archway Tavern and other places near her home.

After doing a few temporary jobs Alison got a job in the Charing Cross branch of Barclay's Bank where she was employed in the back-office staff. To Alison life seemed almost perfect. She had never had a real boyfriend before and John Shaughnessy was the charming Irish lad she had always wished for in her girlish dreams. He was older and more mature than most of the crowd she hung out with but that only added to his attraction. In turn she was a beautiful young woman. She was trusting and almost old fashioned in her attitude to life and love. For her it was simply a matter of falling in love, getting married and having children. She believed in fairy tales. Unfortunately all her wishes for a handsome prince would come true.

It all seemed to be going so well for the couple when John Shaughnessy transferred from his job as a porter to a new job in the clinic as assistant purchasing manager. He was good at what he did; he was efficient and able to work on his own initiative, and he had the happy knack of getting on with most people.

With the new job he also took on the extra task of making sure that the clinic was well supplied with flowers. It made a good impression on the public to have colourful flower arrangements in the corridors and public areas. Almost every day John bought bunches of flowers from a stall outside Waterloo train station which was run by Buster Edwards, the famous Great Train Robber who had done time for one of the most daring crimes of the 1960s, and was now something of a celebrity in the city. John Shaughnessy had the gift of the gab. Even buying flowers became a daily ritual. He would usually chat to Edwards or his assistant for about ten minutes a day, talking about anything from the price of a pint to the complicated rules of the newly fashionable television sport of American football. As a valued customer they wanted to keep him sweet.

When he started working in the purchasing department John Shaughnessy wasn't long meeting up with Michelle Taylor, a tough north London girl who had left school with the most basic qualifications. She might not have been academic but she was bright, a quick learner, and she soon knew the ropes in the department. She too was just eighteen years of age, attractive with long, dark hair and a sassy, confident air for someone who was a petite five feet tall. And she could look after herself. Soon Michelle was referring to John Shaughnessy as her 'Irish charmer' in a couple of notebooks in which she kept a diary of her life.

Shaughnessy took an immediate interest in the attractive Michelle. At first he played a 'fatherly' role, acting as the important assistant purchasing manager helping the junior girl in accounts.

As well as spending about £40 a day at Buster Edwards' stall Shaughnessy also took cuttings from the extensive gardens adjoining the clinic which he arranged in attractive displays. He recruited Michelle Taylor as his assistant. He would either ring her or meet her every day towards the end of that year to discuss the work. At first it was innocent but as they got to know each other better a bond of friendship and attraction began to form between them.

Michelle became ill in January 1989 and had to spend a few days in hospital. Shaughnessy went to visit her, bringing flowers. It made a big impression. When she came back to work he continued ringing her, but now he was chatting her up as they clipped the flowers together. Then one day he asked her out. She had no inkling at the time that he already had a girlfriend and she could hardly contain herself. Returning home where she lived with her parents and her younger sister, Lisa, she innocently announced, 'We're girlfriend and boyfriend.'

After a few dates she found it odd that they never went out together at weekends. During the week it was fine, he would take her to a pub or an Indian restaurant or the pictures. But when it came to the weekends he always seemed to disappear. He told her he had things to do: he was involved in the Irish community and they had meetings and events to go to. She wouldn't be interested, he implied.

One day in March while they were having a meal they talked about sex for the first time. Her tongue loosened a little by the wine, she told him she was a virgin.

'I can do something about that,' he said.

She laughed and they kissed. But she didn't want to rush into anything and neither did John Shaughnessy. He didn't want any little complications in his otherwise perfect double life.

'Are you on the pill?' he asked.

'No,' she answered.

'Well you better go on it,' he said.

That's what she did. That March they had sex for the first time, in his room at the Lambeth Clinic. It happened after they did the flower arranging on a Monday night. Tentative at first, it very quickly became their regular love-making session. Even though they were intimate there was something about John that Michelle couldn't quite figure out. She was never able to penetrate that hard shell which surrounded him. She still didn't suspect she wasn't the only girl in his life.

John Shaughnessy didn't mind the danger, he even seemed to court it. In April 1989, about a month after he started having sex with Michelle Taylor, he went down on his knee and asked nineteen-year-old Alison Blackmore if she would be his bride. Overjoyed, she said yes and they began to plan their wedding. She wanted to buy her wedding dress in Dublin and hold the wedding in her beloved Piltown the following June.

When Michelle first learned about Alison from someone in work, she was livid. But at this stage she didn't know about the engagement and John was able to charm her out of her annoyance. He had never told her he loved her, and neither had she said she loved him. They just enjoyed the sex. Michelle wanted someone to hold her and nobody was better at cuddling up to her than John Shaughnessy. Maybe something would happen to Alison, she reasoned. Maybe he would see sense and fall in love with her. Who could tell! But it did explain his weekend absences. Michelle was jealous at first, but she felt confident she could win the battle for his heart. Soon they were having sex again. Everything went back to normal. John and Michelle even enrolled in night classes together, doing weight training on a Tuesday and aerobics on a Thursday night.

Michelle went away on holidays in September and on her first day back at work someone asked if she'd heard the news.

'No,' she answered.

'John and Alison got engaged, they're going to be married next year.'

She was devastated. But when she confronted John Shaughnessy he simply denied it. 'Why are you wearing that ring?' she sneered.

'Alison gave it to me, she likes me to wear it,' he lied, fingering the ring that marked his new status.

After a few days of getting the cold shoulder he invited her out for a romantic meal and Michelle accepted. In the restaurant he was at his charming best, ordering a good bottle of wine, lulling her into a romantic mood. The wine was poured and they were about to eat the meal he had ordered for the two of them when he turned, looked her in the eye and for once in his life told the truth.

'I have something to confess,' he said, his nervousness bringing out his lush Roscommon brogue.

She looked at him.

'I've got engaged to Alison . . . I'm sorry.'

'You bastard!' she said and she stormed out of the restaurant.

John Shaughnessy sat there for a few moments, a nervous smile playing on his lips. He sipped his wine until the glass was empty then he paid the bill and left. As he walked out he wasn't sure if he was happy or sad.

'I remember telling John what I thought of him. I felt used,' Michelle wrote in her diary later.

For a few weeks afterwards Michelle avoided John at the clinic. If they had to be together she was curt and businesslike. He bided his time.

'I didn't talk to him for a couple of months, but then we drifted back. I didn't go out of my way to encourage him, it just seemed to happen,' she remembered.

She just couldn't resist him. Even if she didn't tell him she loved him, deep down she wanted him so badly she would put up with almost anything just to feel him close to her.

'She was angry . . . but she would always come back again, being a bit forward and things like that,' explained John. He expected it and she had a habit of living up to his expectations.

In her diary Michelle Taylor wrote how John had subtly wooed her back, even though he was now engaged and the marriage had been set for June of the following year.

> He said I hurt him today. He was very angry
> when I said he used me. He kissed me very
> tightly and said I had a small bottom. When I
> don't play putty in his hands he gets very angry.
> I always back down and give in to John. I wish
> deep down this would change.

At one stage they even discussed what it would be like to be married to each other.

'I would say to him that we would not get on if we were married and together all the time,' said Michelle.

By the time Michelle first met Alison Blackmore at the office Christmas party in 1989 she and John Shaughnessy had resumed their clandestine sexual encounters. Surprisingly, the two girls got on well together. There were a few knowing smiles around the room as Michelle and Alison chatted and John played the perfect gentleman, making sure everybody was all right for drinks. After that the threesome started seeing each other socially every so often.

Innocent Alison never suspected a thing, she just thought John and Michelle were the good friends he assured her they were. She accepted that they worked closely together and that it was nice to have somebody to go to the night classes with while she was at home in her parents' house on the other side of London.

But Michelle Taylor was two-faced. While she was being nice to Alison to her face she was writing horrible things in her secret diary.

> I hate Alison, the unwashed bitch . . . the dream
> solution would be for her to disappear . . . and
> then maybe I could give everything to the man I
> love.

But the 'dream solution' didn't happen and Michelle Taylor was sleeping with John Shaughnessy in his hotel bedroom in Kilkenny the night before he was to marry Alison.

The following morning, June 23, 1990, Michelle dressed in her wedding finery and, playing the part of 'his best friend', even drove the groom from Kilkenny out to the village of Piltown where the two-timing Irish charmer married his radiant and trusting bride.

As the wedding video rolled, Michelle Taylor approached the top table where she kissed John Shaughnessy on the lips and congratulated the new Mrs Alison Shaughnessy with a kiss on the cheek.

But while the wedding celebration was a day to remember

the following day, June 24, was like a nightmare. John and Alison woke up to the news that one of their guests, Frank Burke, a first cousin of John Shaughnessy, had been killed when his car crashed as he drove home from the wedding the previous night. His mother, who was with him, was seriously injured. Instead of going on a honeymoon John and Alison had to attend the tragic funeral that followed.

Back in London the couple settled into married life with Alison now moving into John's accommodation adjacent to the Churchill Clinic. Michelle Taylor had also moved into the hostel and was now living in the block next to the newly weds.

Within weeks of his marriage John Shaughnessy and Michelle Taylor eased back into 'flower arranging' and sex on a Monday night. Occasionally, when Alison was staying overnight with her parents, he would stay overnight in Michelle's room at the clinic. He thought nobody knew about the affair. But there are no secrets in a place like that where everybody listens for the slamming of a door and knows who is walking the corridors in the darkness.

In early January 1991 Alison and John moved out of their rooms at the Churchill Clinic and into Flat 3, 41 Vardens Road, Battersea. It was about fifteen to twenty minutes drive from where John worked and about thirty-five minutes by train and bus to Charing Cross where Alison worked in the bank. The tenancy of the flat was passed on to them by John's aunt, the mother of Frank Burke who had been killed driving from their wedding. She couldn't face returning to London where she lived and they were given the keys.

The newly married Alison settled into a routine of work, watching *Coronation Street* on the television, reading and the occasional drink and meal out. She was well liked at work, but she wasn't one of the crew who went to the pub on a Friday night. She occasionally joined them if there was something special on, but her routine was fixed. She left work almost on the dot of 5 p.m. and took the bus and then the train, arriving at her doorstep usually between 5.35 p.m. and 5.40 p.m.

Since the wedding John, Alison and Michelle had got on well socially. They often went out together and one night after an Indian meal they went back to the Shaughnessys' flat to watch television. It was getting late and Alison said she had to be up for work early the following morning; she was tired and she was going to bed.

John and Michelle continued to watch television together. He put his hand out and touched her breast. She pushed it away, feeling uncomfortable with Alison in the next room. He went into the bedroom and came out a moment later.

'She's asleep,' he said.

'He kissed me and kissed me. He started to undress me,' said Michelle, describing the scene. She told him not to.

'Okay,' he replied, 'but give me a kiss.'

They kissed long and passionately as they waited for the taxi to come and take Michelle home.

'I was glad it was me who refused this time,' she said.

By nature Alison was a most trusting person, but then something happened to make her suspect that her husband John and his 'friend' Michelle might be up to more than aerobics. One day as she was going through his jacket, making sure that the pockets were empty before she brought it to the cleaners, she was dismayed to come across what appeared to be a love letter. Even more incriminating were the stubs of two tickets to the romantic comedy *When Harry Met Sally*. Little did Alison know that the famous 'orgasm' scene in the movie was one which her husband regularly played out with his lover, only he was doing it for real.

When she asked him about the letter he laughed and told her it was just a note from one of the patients who was 'a bit cracked'. He said he'd gone to the 'girlie' film with a friend from the clinic 'for a laugh'.

But Alison wasn't convinced. A short time later the Shaughnessys were out for a meal with a group of friends and Alison confided in Michelle that she suspected John was being unfaithful. She may have been testing John's lover or it may have been completely innocent, but in the weeks that followed her suspicions crystalised into a growing dislike of Michelle Taylor. Michelle saw the warning signs.

By March 1991 Michelle had got into the habit of driving John home from the clinic every evening. Some of their colleagues found it bizarre behaviour for a newly married man to fall into the daily routine of having himself driven home by an attractive young woman. But they carried on regardless. It started because he asked her to collect some pots from the flat and he didn't have a car. After that it became part of their day.

Alison said nothing, but she was growing increasingly

resentful and she began to write down her dislike and suspicion of Michelle in a letter she was writing to a friend in Ireland.

On a sunny hot day in London between 5.30 and 5.45 p.m. Alison Shaughnessy, wearing a T-shirt and sweater, a denim jacket and a floral print skirt, would have entered her apartment in Vardens Road. It was Monday, June 3, 1991, just twenty days from her first wedding anniversary. Apart from the incident with the love letter and the tickets for the movie, marriage had been a joy to Alison. It was always difficult learning to live with someone but she was young and she and John generally got on well together. Now that they had their own place it was getting easier.

Lately they had even begun talking about having a family. Alison was only twenty-one but she loved babies and children. She wouldn't mind giving up her job at the bank if they were to have a child. John suggested they might move over to Ireland; it would be better for the child and he could easily get a job in a hotel or some place like that.

Alison emerged from her reverie at the outer doorway of the flats: there were visitors waiting for her. They exchanged hellos and she opened the outer door. Alison knew them well enough and she knew they wouldn't be staying long so she didn't lock it, although John had always warned her about that. She opened the door to Flat 3 and walked up another flight of steps. Suddenly a knife flashed, its silver blade glinting in the evening sunlight. Alison put up her arm to defend herself but the blade kept coming down, the knife penetrating her flesh. She was stabbed and stabbed – twenty-four times – and then the blade slashed across her windpipe, severing an artery in her neck and cutting off her air supply. She stood for maybe four seconds, bleeding and gasping for air, and then, as her life ebbed away, she buckled, sprawling on the floor on her stomach. Her attacker leaned over her prone body and began to stab and stab another thirty times into her back. When the blood-frenzy was over the killer walked out pulling the door closed, but leaving it unlocked.

Dr Michael Unsworth-White, a consultant surgeon, was cycling down Vardens Road at about 5.45 p.m. when he saw two girls running down the steps of one of the houses and along the street. One girl had a carrier bag, he noted. He cycled on, the incident floating to the back of his mind.

As the surgeon was passing by his house, John Shaughnessy was buying flowers at Buster Edwards' stall. He was there for ten minutes and that day they discussed American football. Apart from buying flowers for the clinic he also bought a bunch to bring home to Alison. He went back to the clinic and had a cup of tea with Michelle Taylor, who had had a long day. She had by now switched jobs at the clinic, moving from the accounts department to evening work as a housekeeper, working four nights a week. This allowed her to work for her father who had a floor-cleaning business. She had been up at 5.30 that morning to help her father with a cleaning job in a local shopping centre, followed by another at a fire station. After an hour at home at lunchtime with her mother she had gone shopping in Bromley with her sister Lisa, who was looking for a party dress. Later they were seen by one of the receptionists as they drove into the clinic minutes after 6 p.m. in their Ford Sierra estate car. Lisa had followed in her sister's footsteps and also worked in the clinic.

That evening John and Michelle organised the flower arrangements as usual. At about 8 o'clock Michelle called into the room where Lisa was playing Monopoly with their friend JJ, Jeanette Tapp the housekeeping assistant. She had a glass of water and a cigarette and said she was going to leave John home, as she usually did. They left in her white Ford Sierra car at about 8.15 p.m., arriving at the flat about fifteen minutes later.

John Shaughnessy walked up the steps, followed by Michelle, and found the outer door closed, but unlocked. He thought it was unusual. Carrying the bunch of flowers for Alison, he went in his own door and up the second set of steps. At the top of the steps near the toilet door, he saw Alison lying on the floor.

'Alison, Alison,' he wailed.

Michelle Taylor ran up and, kneeling down, put her hand under Alison Shaughnessy's head. She was stiff, and a dribble of blood – now dry – ran from her mouth. But for someone who had been stabbed fifty-four times there was surprisingly little blood around the place. The wounds were mostly shallow and her clothes had soaked up the rest of it.

Realising that Alison was dead Michelle Taylor went into the bathroom and washed her hands, which had become smeared with blood. Then she ran out of the apartment and went across the street to a bar. The alarm was immediately raised and a London transport policeman took charge of the scene until the police and detectives arrived.

'I don't know what happened, I don't know what happened,' repeated John Shaughnessy in a daze.

Pathologist Rufus Crompton told police he believed Alison Shaughnessy was probably killed by a woman wielding a sharp knife, about five inches long. The force of the blows suggested this. Who could it be?

When Michelle Taylor was questioned in detail the first time she did not at first admit that she was having an affair with John Shaughnessy. However, she told detectives about two other affairs she believed he had engaged in while he was going out with Alison. The first was with an Irish girl called Natalie McGuinness who, Michelle said, was from Roscommon. She also told police about a girl called Cathy whom he had gone to see in New York and who had been his lover when he was going out with Alison. Michelle was particularly jealous of one girl who was said to keep a T-shirt of John's under her pillow to remind her of their encounter.

Police were puzzled. They not only found Michelle Taylor's prints in the Shaughnessys' apartment, but they also found prints of her younger sister Lisa. But Lisa Taylor had never been to the apartment – John Shaughnessy said so. So how had her fingerprints been found just inside the door? There was only one explanation. She had to have been there on the day of the murder. The police fingerprint expert was certain that her prints were fresh, put there in the forty-eight hours before Alison was so brutally murdered.

But the Taylor girls had an alibi, and it was cast iron. Their friend JJ swore to the police that they had been in her room at the clinic from 5 o'clock that evening and had stayed there for some time. The girls had also been seen by witnesses entering the Churchill Clinic at 6.08 p.m., twenty-three minutes after the murder of Alison Shaughnessy. Could they have left the clinic without being seen, murdered Alison, changed out of blood-spattered clothes and got from the flat in Vardons Road to the Churchill Clinic in fifteen or twenty minutes? It was unlikely.

In an interview three days after the murder John Shaughnessy admitted having an affair with Michelle Taylor, telling police that it had ended ten weeks before the murder. The details were sketchy at this stage, but police began to suspect that the murder of Alison Shaughnessy was a crime of passion rather than a random attack.

On June 20, after a series of memorial services in London, Alison Shaughnessy's body was brought back to Ireland for burial. John Shaughnessy was making the same journey he had made with his bride-to-be a year earlier. There was a huge crowd at the removal that evening and twenty-one-year-old Alison Shaughnessy was buried the following morning in Piltown churchyard, two days short of her first wedding anniversary in the very same village. Dressed in sombre black, John Shaughnessy played the part of the grieving widower to perfection. He probably was deeply traumatised by the murder of his young bride but even as he buried his wife he knew his affair with Michelle Taylor was central to the murder investigation. He didn't have much time to think about it on his own, however.

A little more than a week after the funeral John Shaughnessy got a call from Michelle Taylor. After asking each other how they were she got to the point.

'I want to see you,' she said.

'I won't be back for another while,' he replied.

'I'm in Ireland, can I come down?'

He said she could.

Before the murder Michelle Taylor had planned a holiday in Ireland with an Irish friend from the clinic, intending to stay with the girl's parents. But once she arrived in Ireland she made the phone call to John and left her friend, heading to Roscommon to stay in a hotel with her lover.

Michelle went back to England on July 7, and on July 20 John Shaughnessy returned with Alison's parents. John and Michelle's absence in Ireland had caused a certain amount of difficulty for detectives investigating the murder. They began a series of witness interviews with John Shaughnessy and Michelle Taylor to confirm the unsavoury details established from those who knew what was going on in the Churchill Clinic. But Michelle and Lisa Taylor's alibi held firm.

The detective in charge of the investigation directed that no details of the sexual relationship between Shaughnessy and Taylor should get out. He did not want the lurid details to become public knowledge if their sexual transgressions had nothing to do with the murder of Alison.

In the meantime Barclay's Bank, where Alison Shaughnessy had worked, offered a reward for information leading to her killer. It was then that the cycling surgeon Dr Michael Unsworth-White came forward with information to the police. At first he said he saw two girls running down the steps of the flat, one White and one Black. But later he changed his mind and agreed that they had both been White, although he was unable to pick out either of the Taylor sisters from a police line-up. But detectives were firmly convinced that it had to be them. Everything pointed to it: the surgeon could identify two girls at the scene; Lisa Taylor's fingerprints confirmed her presence; the jealousy and hatred that Michelle Taylor had for Alison Shaughnessy was clear from witness statements and confirmed in the wire-back notebooks where Michelle had written her diary. All they had to do was crack the alibi.

Early in the morning of August 7, 1990, Michelle Taylor, Lisa Taylor and Jeanette 'JJ' Tapp were arrested and taken to different police stations in London to be questioned.

Within an hour Jeanette Tapp withdrew her alibi for the sisters after she was charged with conspiracy to commit murder. She told detectives that in fact she had been out shopping on the Monday that Alison Shaughnessy was murdered and hadn't arrived back at her room in the clinic until after 7 p.m. Lisa Taylor was waiting for her there and told her that she and Michelle had been there since 5 p.m. When she was questioned the day after the murder, JJ told detectives that the sisters were in her room at 5 p.m., making it impossible for them to have killed Alison.

Now, questioned for the second time, JJ was afraid to change her story and repeated the lie. But faced with being dragged into a murder prosecution herself she was forced to tell the truth.

Previously, Michelle and Lisa Taylor had been questioned as witnesses to the murder of Alison Shaughnessy. But now with their alibi in tatters they were under arrest on suspicion of murder. They were questioned throughout the day and held overnight. The following day, August 8 at 3.10 p.m., Michelle and Lisa Taylor were charged with the murder of Alison Shaughnessy.

Their trial at the Old Bailey in July 1992 was a sensational event as details of John Shaughnessy's sexual exploits were outlined in graphic detail. Asked to explain her entry: 'I hate Alison, the unwashed bitch', Michelle Taylor portrayed herself as a young woman used by an unscrupulous older man.

> When I wrote that I was very depressed because of the affair I was having with John. I wanted to be friends with Alison but I could not because I was having an affair with her husband. I was confused about my feelings at the time. I felt John was using me, but I felt he cared for me.

Later she even analysed her own shifting emotions.

> As time went on I realised it was not Alison I hated, but John.

Prosecutors claimed that Michelle Taylor was obsessed with John Shaughnessy and that when she realised he was going to return to Ireland with Alison to start a family she decided the only way to prevent this was to kill her love rival. She recruited her sister and the two of them carried out the frenzied attack on Alison Shaughnessy. The jury accepted this theory and the two sisters were found guilty of the murder of the beautiful twenty-one-year-old.

But less than a year later, on June 11, 1993, Michelle and Lisa Taylor were freed by the appeal court which overturned the conviction. It was declared unsafe because Dr Unsworth-White's statement, describing one of the girls as Black, had been withheld from the defence team acting for the Taylor sisters, and it was also revealed that the surgeon was now seeking to be paid the reward offered by Barclay's Bank.

But another major factor was what Lord Justice McGowan called 'prejudicial reporting of the trial in the press'.

> What the press did was not reporting at all, it was comment and comment which assumed the guilt of the two girls in the dock.

He ordered that they could not be re-tried because they would not get a fair trial.

That evening Michelle and Lisa Taylor popped open a bottle of champagne in their parents' home in north London.

Alison Shaughnessy's parents were 'shocked and devastated' by the verdict. They kept their feelings to themselves, however. While John Shaughnessy has been seen walking down the street in Killarney, Co Kerry, arm in arm with a woman, Alison's parents walk up the roadway near Piltown where they now live to visit their daughter's grave.

Inscribed on Alison's tombstone is the legend:

Love's last gift – remembrance.

Erected by her husband John.

13

THE BUTCHER BOY

He was shuffling around the waste ground opposite the shop in Milltown in Co Kildare earlier that day. It was a cold, sleety January afternoon and when someone asked him what he was doing he said he'd lost a ten pound note. He stayed there, staring at the ground moving stones with his foot, and then looking up and gazing across the road.

He was twenty-four years old without much in his life. He had been apprenticed to a butcher and knew how to carve a piece of flesh with the blade of a newly sharpened boning knife. But he didn't like the job. He just didn't seem able to get on with other people and so he left, even though he didn't have another job to go to.

He was on the dole. He couldn't stand the ordered life of getting up in the morning, going to work, coming home tired and plonking himself in front of the television. Where was the sense in that? Now he spent his days shuffling around the house, watching videos. It was an aimless sort of existence.

He had kept one of the butcher's knives. It was in a bag upstairs under some clothes in the wardrobe. He didn't know why he kept it, it was just the feel of the handle, the weight of it in his hand, the power of the flashing steel in his powerless, aimless life.

But there was something else in his life that he kept hidden, a dream of his that he told nobody about. In the cold half-light of a winter's afternoon he was dreaming of the warmth of a woman . . . but not just any woman. He could see her moving around inside the shop. But he couldn't touch her. He wanted to; he wanted to possess her. But he knew he never could. That was just the way it was. She hardly noticed him, even when he looked into her big, sparkling green eyes. It would only last for a moment, a fleeting second of pleasure, then his glance would fall away. He wouldn't be able to maintain eye contact. He didn't have the confidence.

She wasn't one of those young girls he saw around the village flaunting themselves. They weren't real women. 'Young girls with nothing in their jeans/but pretty blue wishes and sweet little dreams' as Tom Waits sang. No, the woman he fantasised about was a mature woman of the world. She smiled in a knowing way, but she didn't smile for him. He was just another customer.

That could change, at the point of a butcher's knife.

He remembered reading about Brendan O'Donnell, the man who murdered Imelda Riney and her three-year-old son, Liam, and the priest, Fr Joe Walshe, in the woods in Co Clare a few years before. He was dead now, but for those few days he had set the lakeshore around Mountshannon alight and everybody had been glued to the papers finding out about his evil deeds.

They were alike in ways. Loners and outcasts, yet driven to

leave their mark, to live their obsessions and suffer the consequences, whatever these might be.

O'Donnell didn't seem to have had a plan. He lived wild in the woods, his russet beard and his green clothes giving him camouflage as he moved along familiar paths among the tall trees where the light didn't penetrate. He was known and unknown. He was feared, but never feared enough – until he exploded without warning in a blood lust, engulfing all he touched.

Then there was the woman, Imelda Riney. He had seen the pictures in the newspapers. A beautiful woman, wearing a big sun hat with a wide brim and that long straw-coloured hair streaming over her shoulders. Living in her cottage in the woods she was happy with her two children, finding peace in her painting and her seclusion. But she was powerless in the strong arms of Brendan O'Donnell.

O'Donnell stood out because of his wild eyes and his killing ways. But every town in Ireland has a version of Brendan O'Donnell. Most of them carry on relatively normal lives although they might be seen as outsiders and oddities. They hide their obsessions in drink or drugs or porn. Mostly they don't look different from anyone else walking down Main Street in the rain – he knew he didn't. But inside he felt different. He had this urge that wasn't normal. It was the urge to destroy. It just takes something to trigger it. The longing becomes unbearable. The dark winter evening closes in and something cracks. It's not like that for normal people who can control how they feel most of them time. He was just waiting to explode, all it needed was the spark – and that flared in the dim winter light. He could feel it. He could wait no longer.

He flicked a stone with his trainer and felt the cold, biting wind and the rain soak through his thin tracksuit top and he turned and walked towards home.

The Store was Joyce Quinn's little dream. Milltown was once a stopping point for canal barges chugging through the flat Kildare countryside. But all that was long in the past. Now it's just a huddle of houses around a humpy bridge, a pub and the shop. There's an old graveyard at the back of the shop and that January afternoon in the sleet and the rain it was hard to imagine that The Store was Joyce Quinn's dream come true.

Brought up in Dublin, Joyce's father, Commandant Tommy Wickham, was a senior officer in the Irish army. When she was a teenager he was shot dead by two Syrians in the Golan Heights while on duty with the United Nations peacekeepers in 1967.

It was another senseless killing. He was trying to keep the peace and they shot him dead for it, thousands of miles from home and the ones he loved. When Tommy Wickham went to Syria he was a bit like a missionary entering the dark continent. He had volunteered because he thought that was what army life was about, going to war zones. But he hadn't gone to fight, he had gone in peace in the weeks after the first Arab/Israeli war. He was paid £1 a day for his troubles and in the end he came back to Ireland in a coffin. It was a huge family tragedy.

But ironically his daughter Joyce ended up marrying Ray Quinn, who himself would rise to the rank of commandant in the Irish army. In a further irony his path in life would also lead them to the Middle East to the very country where Joyce's father was killed.

It was there, amid the minarets and the souks and the exotic locations and the ex-pats who made up the United Nations force, that Ray and Joyce Quinn began to talk about what they would do when they got back to Ireland after the two-year tour of duty.

Joyce Quinn had worked in the Blood Bank when she left school but in those days when you married you had to leave your job. She didn't have a choice and now she regretted it. She also left Dublin, moving to Kildare where they started a family almost immediately.

It was a good life and a fulfilling one too. They were very happily married and were soon the parents of three beautiful children, Nicole, David and Lisa. As they grew up Joyce Quinn no longer felt her life was fulfilled. She saw many of the younger women in the close-knit army group who had time on their hands start their own businesses or take on jobs.

Sitting beneath the beating sun of Syria Joyce Quinn said that when they got back home she wouldn't mind starting her own business with the money they accumulated. In the early 1990s her little dream began to take flight.

'The shop came up for sale and we bought it,' said Ray Quinn.

The couple and their three children lived comfortably in

Moortown near Kildare and Joyce Quinn drove out every day in her Citroen car to open the shop.

There was a bit of passing trade but Milltown is a backwater between the busy towns of Naas, Newbridge and Kildare. Most of the time the business came from people in Millview, the council estate across the road, where people used it as a convenience store to supplement their other shopping. It was a steady business selling newspapers, sweets and such like but the hours were long and standing on her feet most of the day left her fatigued.

'I am so tired, remind me to go to bed early tonight,' she told her husband that morning before she set off in the drizzling rain to open up The Store.

In the afternoon she left her eldest daughter Nicole to mind the shop and she drove home to put on the meat for the dinner. After everything was arranged and the vegetables prepared she drove back out to the shop.

At about 6.15 p.m. Ray Quinn called in on his way from work. It was Budget Day in Dáil Éireann and he picked up the Evening Herald from the counter and began to scan the headlines, looking to see if there was anything happening in Defence or Justice.

Comdt. Ray Quinn was based in Kildare and his job was to liaise with the gardaí on major events, such as the visit of foreign dignitaries or joint operations involving police and army personnel. Because of his job he was very security conscious. He was always careful himself and he knew that his wife could be vulnerable with the takings from the shop, especially travelling the lonely back roads between Milltown and their home in Kildare. Part of her journey would take her across the Curragh plain, a big expanse of open space without houses for miles.

After an incident one evening when Joyce's car hit a particularly vicious pothole and she was stranded with no way to call for help on a lonely road, he bought her one of the new mobile phones which were just then coming on the market. The first number he saved onto it was the local police station in Kildare.

He also got her a can of Mace, an anti-attack spray that is widely available in America but is not really in use in Ireland. Sprayed on an assailant it blinds them, giving the person who is attacked time to flee. Joyce Quinn kept the can in her shoulder bag. She had never had to use it.

In truth Ray Quinn didn't really expect anything to happen. The shop was steady but it was hardly a goldmine or a target for armed robbers. After four years Joyce knew most of the people in the local community, who depended on her for credit when they hadn't got the cash to pay for something essential like a bottle of milk or a loaf of bread.

'Don't put on the vegetables until after seven, I want them nice and crispy,' she warned her husband, as he stood in the back of the shop reading through the sketchy details of the budget in the paper.

Ray told his daughter Nicole to 'come on' and said something mundane like 'see you' as he left the shop and headed for his own car to drive back home. Outside it was dark and wet. It wasn't a night for anyone to be out. The village seemed deserted, even the pub next door didn't look like it was thriving that night.

Joyce Quinn normally closed the shop at 7 p.m., giving people coming home from work time to call in for some item they might need. It was a ten- to fifteen-minute drive back to the house depending on the traffic. Ray Quinn didn't expect his wife to be far behind him.

While she was waiting to close up, Joyce counted out the cash takings for the day. There was a little more than £300 and she packed it into her cash box. There were no customers lingering so shortly after 6.45 p.m., knowing that there was unlikely to be anybody coming, she closed the shop a few minutes early. She walked out into the rain locked the door from the outside and pulled down and bolted the metal shutters.

She pressed the home number on her mobile as she walked to the car.

'Put the vegetables on, I'm coming home.'

It was a nice feeling. She liked the thought of a nice dinner and an early night. She walked to her car, put the cash box in the front seat and sat in behind the wheel.

She was pulling out when just down the road she saw a figure in the headlights. It appeared to be a man. He had his arm out, thumbing a lift.

It was dark now. She didn't really have time to think. Instinctively she brought the car to a halt. In a small place where everyone knows everyone else it wouldn't do to pass someone on the road, especially on a chilly, miserable January night, the sort of night 'you wouldn't let a dog out' as the locals would say.

But you had to be careful. Jo Jo Dullard, a young girl thumbing a lift through Co Kildare on her way home to Carlow, just disappeared off the face of the earth over the other side of the county. In another case a couple of years later a young girl almost made it home to her street – just to disappear as if she had been abducted by aliens.

If thoughts of missing women raced through Joyce Quinn's head it was just for a moment because even in the dim light she thought she recognised the person standing in the rain, waiting patiently for a lift.

Any car could have come along, it just happened to be her. Or so she thought. But she was wrong. This was no random act. It had been carefully planned. He had waited, concealed in the hedge, watching her close and lock up, watching her body arch as she pulled down the shutters. He had been waiting for this moment with Joyce Quinn, his moment with destiny.

She stopped and opened the door.

Joyce Quinn was relieved to see that she did indeed know him. He came in and out of the shop. She knew his family too. She gave them credit. He was a bit funny, he never said very much and he never met her eyes when he asked for something. But she knew him and that was a relief. It would only take ten or fifteen minutes to get him to Kildare where he was going and then she would be going home to a cosy dinner and an early night.

A lot of people admired Joyce Quinn. At the age of forty-four she was still a very attractive woman. She was tall and slim, she had a wide smile and an easy manner when she met people. She dressed well and enjoyed life. She had been married for twenty-three years and she still loved her husband. Her kids were her pride and joy.

Back in their comfortable home, Ray Quinn and the children waited. Joyce didn't arrive, as they expected. As the vegetables simmered he began to worry. Could something have happened, an accident on the road? Or could she have met somebody and stopped to chat? Unlikely, he thought.

He didn't want to panic but he rang her mobile phone. All he got was the monotone pre-recorded message that told him it was out of coverage and 'Please try again.' All sorts of things ran through his head. The Blood Bank was taking donations of blood over in Newbridge, and Joyce, remembering back to her days working there, always gave a donation when they were in the neighbourhood. But she hadn't said anything. That was unlike her.

Ray Qunn was a man of action. At 7.15 p.m. when she still hadn't arrived he called his son David, then sixteen, and said they would go out to Milltown to see if her car had broken down or if there was some sort of delay. The two girls stayed behind in the house one of them keeping an eye on the dinner and the other on the phone.

As they drove along Ray's experienced eyes scanned the oncoming traffic. Nothing. He looked for signs of someone broken down. Nothing. They got to Milltown. Nothing. The Store was shut, the metal grille locked in place. There was no sign of anything unusual.

He drove out the Newbridge Road, but knew that Joyce would not have gone to the Blood Bank without telling him. He began to drive on the smaller roads that criss-cross the Curragh and are not well known or sign-posted but which he knew like the back of his hand from driving between the barracks in Kildare and the army camp in the Curragh.

The minutes were turning into hours and still no sign. He rang the house on his mobile. No news. Now he was beginning to panic, this was totally out of character.

He went back to Milltown and he and sixteen-year-old David got out of the car. They went around the back to take a look. Ray Quinn was looking for signs that someone had tried to get into the shop and might have kidnapped his wife. David had a small flashlight and in the dark and the rain it gave off a poor beam of light. But there was enough to guide him. He went through a gate at the back and into the small Church of Ireland graveyard with its overgrown paths, leaning headstones and dripping ivy.

Nothing.

As they slipped and scrambled among the headstones Ray Quinn was using all his army training to control his panic. Other people might have found it odd that he would be so worried, but they were a family of routine and all his training told him that people rarely break that sort of routine unless there's a very good reason. Or unless there is nothing they can do about it. He knew he had every right to be worried.

They crossed over the road to the national school and then David Quinn's beam of light picked out the outline of the Citroen car hidden behind one of the buildings. He shouted and his father came running. The rain was trickling down the windscreen and Ray Quinn wrenched open the unlocked door without waiting to peer in.

The empty cash box was thrown on the seat. With the weak beam of the torch they could see the bloodstains smeared on the upholstery.

Ray Quinn let out a howl of anguish.

They were out of Milltown and driving along through the open plain of the Curragh when he ordered Joyce to turn on to a side road. At first she may not have known what would happen, she may have thought he just wanted to be dropped somewhere out there, off the beaten track. He said it was the road to a friend's house and he would be very grateful, rather than having to walk in the rain.

Maybe there was a sense of panic and dread as they drove in the darkness. She would have tried to control it. That was her nature. The first thought that probably struck her was that he wanted the money. But that was impossible, how did he think he was going to get away with it when she knew who he was.

But it wasn't the money. It would have been so much easier if that was all that he wanted. He wanted her.

They searched all through the night. First they combed the

village and then gradually the search widened out onto the Curragh itself. Although it is completely flat there are huge stands of gorse on the plain and it is easy enough to hide something there. All night they hoped that maybe Joyce had somehow survived.

In the dim early morning light soldiers from the army barracks joined the search and some of the locals on horses cantered over the short-cropped plain hoping for some sighting. They still didn't know if robbery was the motive, although the cash was gone. It was unlikely that someone would be kidnapped or harmed for a mere £300.

As the hours wore on and exhaustion set in all Ray Quinn could think about was Joyce and the other women who had disappeared and never been seen again. For a time it seemed that his agony was going to drag on forever like so many other families whose loved ones have never been found. By 10 a.m. he and the three children were exhausted from worry and the long night of searching.

He was told to go home and try to prepare himself to do a public appeal for information. It's a desperate act, but it's something that has to be done.

Only fifteen hours had passed, yet in that short space of time Ray Quinn's normal life had been transformed. Everything he had taken for granted had been snatched away and something so precious was lost. He may have hoped in some tiny part of his mind that it would work out, but realistically he knew that he was never going to see his wife alive again.

Then the doorbell rang.

A senior policeman was standing there. They knew each other. Tears were streaming down the police officer's face. Joyce's body had been found, concealed in a clump of furze just yards from the road Ray had travelled the night before in his desperate search.

At first there was talk of a French man or a foreigner in the shop just before it closed, but as detectives analysed the murder of Joyce Quinn they knew that robbery was only an incidental part of it. She had been stalked. She had been lured into giving her murderer a lift and then she had been raped and murdered.

Rape is such a heinous crime. Followed by murder it usually indicates that the person who carried it out knows the victim or suspects that they will be able to identify them. He had to be local.

But Joyce Quinn wasn't just raped and killed. She was stabbed, then raped while she was either dying or dead, then she was stabbed again. It was appalling abuse by a particularly twisted pervert.

Kenneth O'Reilly, twenty-four, was an unemployed butcher who lived in the Millview Estate about 300 metres away from The Store. He and his family regularly used the shop and were on good terms with Joyce Quinn. He was one of those people who didn't draw attention to himself. About medium height with brown hair he was thin and his only distinguishing feature was a weak blond moustache on his upper lip.

That Tuesday night he was freshly washed and dressed when he arrived at The Milltown Inn for a few drinks with his girlfriend. He didn't drink that much, just a couple of beers, and then he took his girlfriend for a Chinese meal in Kildare. They didn't often do that kind of thing; he was on the dole and there wasn't a lot of spare cash. But that night he seemed to have more money than usual. Word of the search for Joyce Quinn went around the pub, but he didn't seem to pay any attention, or even indicate that he was aware something was going on. He and his girlfriend sat in the corner and didn't say very much.

In the days that followed Kenneth O'Reilly settled back into his routine, watching videos, hanging around, having the occasional drink. The Store was closed; he couldn't call there any more.

But he was being watched. Detectives had latched onto the loner – they had asked about anyone who regularly used the shop. They were interested in the butcher. They were very interested to know if he had a knife.

They raided the house and found it upstairs, wrapped up in a bag at the bottom of the wardrobe: a long butcher's blade. It was the weapon used to kill Joyce Quinn.

But the twisted killer Kenneth O'Reilly wasn't going to make it easy for anyone. Although he admitted to detectives that he killed Joyce Quinn, he came up with the improbable story that it was in self-defence. He claimed that when he sat into the car she had driven off the by-road and suddenly produced the knife and attempted to attack him.

Joyce Quinn's three children examined the long blade and said they had never seen it before.

When the trial of Kenneth O'Reilly opened in the Central Criminal Court in Dublin, it lasted just a few minutes longer than Joyce Quinn's final journey. Kenneth O'Reilly said 'Guilty' when asked how he pleaded. It was only the second word that Ray Quinn ever heard from his mouth. The other was a muttered 'sorry' at one of his court appearances.

His barrister, Patrick McEntee SC, said that O'Reilly's plea was unambiguous and there was no reason for anything further to be said.

That short, dark journey from Joyce Quinn's little shop in Milltown to the scene of her brutal murder remains a mystery. Whatever triggered such a foul crime against a beautiful and innocent woman is stowed away in the dark recesses of Kenneth O'Reilly's mind. He chose not to bare his soul.

So the torment continues. Despite the appalling nature of the murder, Joyce's husband really did want to know what happened that night and why it happened. He wasn't afraid of the dark secret. But Kenneth O'Reilly wouldn't give him that little bit of satisfaction – because maybe it was just too unpleasant for even his twisted mind to bear.